BOOKS BY IRVING CHERNEV

CHESSBOARD MAGIC

WINNING CHESS TRAPS

THE RUSSIANS PLAY CHESS

THE BRIGHT SIDE OF CHESS

INVITATION TO CHESS
(with *Kenneth Harkness*)

BOOKS BY FRED REINFELD

CHESS BY YOURSELF

CHALLENGE TO CHESSPLAYERS

THE IMMORTAL GAMES OF CAPABLANCA

CHESS MASTERY BY QUESTION AND ANSWER

LEARN CHESS FAST!
(with *Sammy Reshevsky*)

Winning
CHESS

by Irving Chernev
and Fred Reinfeld

*Methodical thinking is of more use in chess
than inspiration —* PURDY

19 48

SIMON AND SCHUSTER

ISBN: 978-1-5011-1758-9

MANUFACTURED IN THE UNITED STATES OF AMERICA
BY KINGSPORT PRESS, INC., KINGSPORT, TENN.

The Language of Chess

CHESS NOTATION is as useful as the alphabet, and much easier to learn. It is the magic key that opens the door to the entire wealth of chess literature. By its use you can play over the exciting games of the masters for sheer pleasure, or study their comments on the various moves to improve your own playing ability. Notation is simply a brief way of describing what happens on the chessboard—where the pieces move, or what captures they make. These are the symbols for the pieces:

King	K
Queen	Q
Rook	R
Bishop	B
Knight	Kt
Pawn	P

The pieces at the right of the King are called the King Bishop, the King Knight and the King Rook. Abbreviated, they are KB, KKt and KR. The pieces on the Queen's left are, in chess shorthand, QB, QKt and QR. The Pawns too, are given distinctive names. Starting at the left, the Pawn in front of the Queen Rook (QR) is the Queen Rook Pawn (QRP). At its right is the Queen Knight Pawn (QKtP), then the Queen Bishop Pawn (QBP) etc.

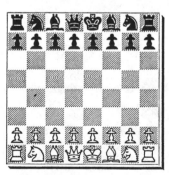

The pieces set up at the beginning of a game. The bottom row from left to right is the first rank. The White Pawns stand on the second rank. The row above the second rank is the third rank, and so on to the last row, which is the eighth rank.

All the squares on the first rank are square one (1). Thus, the QR stands at QR1, the QKt is on QKt1, the QB on QB1, etc. All the Pawns occupy square two (2). The QRP stands on QR2, the QKtP is on QKt2, the QBP on QB2, the QP on Q2, the KP on K2, etc. Suppose we moved the KP two squares as our first move, how would we describe this move in chess notation? We could write it **KP—K4** (which would be read, King Pawn to King four). The full name of the Pawn, though, would be unnecessary, as no other Pawn but the King Pawn could go to K4. The move should then be written **P—K4**. The four is clear: it is the fourth square on the row of squares starting from K1. One more thing remains in recording a move, and that is its number. Since this is White's first move, it is scored this way: *1* **P—K4.**

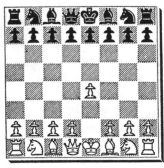

Position after *1* P—K4. *The row of squares on which the KP stands leading from K1 to K8 is called a file. The files are named after the pieces occupying the first rank. The Pawn therefore stands on the King file.*

A few more abbreviations, and we will be ready to follow a game score. *Check* is shortened to *ch;* a capture is scored by an x (PxP means Pawn takes, i.e. captures Pawn); a capture *en passant* is *e.p. Castling* on the *King-side* is indicated by **O—O**, while *Queen-side castling* is written **O—O—O.** Replace the King Pawn at his original square (K2), and we will try reading a chess short story:

WHITE	BLACK
R. Reti	*S. Tartakover*
1 **P—K4**	**P—QB3**

Notice that *Black counts from his side of the board.* The square QB3 from Black's side of the board is QB6 from White's side. It is unnecessary to specify which Pawn goes to QB3, as only the QBP can move there.

| 2 P—Q4 | P—Q4 |
| 3 Kt—QB3 | PxP |

White's and Black's second moves are clear, as in each case only one Pawn (the QP) could go to Q4. White's third move distinguished between his two Knights. Had the move read *3 Kt—B3,* it might have been interpreted as a move of the King Knight which can also go to a B3. Black's third move would be read Pawn takes Pawn, the "x" signifying a capture. It can hardly be misunderstood, as only one of his Pawns can capture an enemy Pawn, and only one of White's Pawns can be captured by a Pawn. Compare the position on your board with the next diagram.

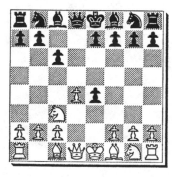

Position after Black's third move. *Note that Black has two Pawns on his King file. In switching to the King file, Black's Queen Pawn now becomes a King Pawn.*

| 4 KtxP | Kt—B3 |

Excess description is omitted. White's Knight could have captured only one Pawn, the KP. Black did not specify which Knight should go to B3. Only his KKt could have gone there. Nor is it necessary to say which B3, as QB3 is occupied by a Pawn.

5 Q—Q3   P—K4
6 PxP   Q—R4ch
7 B—Q2   QxKP

This is the state of affairs:

It would be misleading to record Black's last move as . . . QxP, as he could have captured White's QRP. The move might be silly on account of the reply 8 RxQ, but it is a legal move.

8 O—O—O   KtxKt

The position now deserves a diagram, as White's next move is startling.

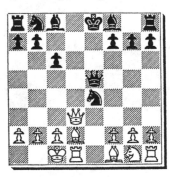

White forces a mate in three moves, beginning with a beautiful Queen sacrifice.

9   Q—Q8ch!!   KxQ
10 B—Kt5 dbl ch   K—K1
11 R—Q8 mate

Had Black on his last move chosen his only alternative to escape the double check and moved his King to B2, White would have finished him with *11 B—B8* mate.

Table of Contents

How to Use This Book to Advantage—
Your Advantage

♞ EVERY CHESSPLAYER, from beginner to expert, asks the same question: *"How can I improve my game?"* In our earnest endeavor to find the best possible answer, we have studied over 50,000 games played in tournaments and matches from 1851 to the present day by the greatest chess masters. This intensive research confirmed what we had long suspected: *the proper use of combination play is the secret of winning chess.*

Tactical methods may lead directly to checkmate. In the vast majority of cases, however, combination play is used *as a means of winning material*—a piece or a Pawn. In a game between players of equal strength, the advantage of a piece (where no freak factors are present) is enough to force immediate resignation; the chances of saving the game with such inferior forces are infinitesimal. The advantage of a Pawn is also conclusive, although, to be sure, it allows a far more stubborn resistance. For clarity's sake, all the positions in this book where gain of material is the goal, are so clean-cut that the opponent has no compensation for the lost material.

Combinations can be broken down into simple, basic, easily recognizable elements, for example *the pin, the Knight fork, the double attack, the discovered check, the double check.* Each of these devices has certain distinguishing characteristics, repetitive patterns which announce its presence on the chessboard.

But these patterns are useful only to those for whom they have a meaning—those who know what to look for! An instance: the chapter on *the pin* teaches you to look for a pin the moment that the opponent's King and Queen are in direct line with each other—whether that line is a file, rank or diagonal. The *technique* of exploiting the pin (by adding pressure on the pinned piece, or driving off its defenders, or undermining its support by exchanges etc.) is discussed and illustrated by the use of simple, *decisive* positions taken from *actual play.*

As each chapter proceeds to its conclusion, the examples become progressively more difficult. But, paradoxically enough, you may find the "difficult" positions unexpectedly easy because by that time you will be completely familiar with the theme under discussion. Once you can apply these tactical methods with confidence, it will become instinctive to anticipate opportunities for employing them; using single themes or blending a number of them, you will be on the way to playing winning chess.

The tactical motifs have been arranged in the order of frequency with which they occur in practical play. The most important single device by which games are won is the pin, or the threat of a pin. Therefore the pin has been given pride of place. *The frequency with which a theme is employed is of course the key to its usefulness.*

We have tried to use simple language throughout, so that the player who knows little beyond the rules of the game and the moves of the pieces, will not be mystified by technical terms. *We have deliberately employed repetition.* Such maxims as "Remember the priority of check!" or "Look at every possible capture! It cuts down your opponent's choice of replies," will be encountered frequently. This is done to instil in the reader the habit of picturing *forcing* combinations, as the master does.

The illustrative positions have been picked for entertainment *and* instruction. These positions are generally so simple that they can be followed mentally from the diagrams. Played over this way, they will make pleasant reading, for there is something irresistibly fascinating about a combination.

But that is not the way to learn how to be a better chessplayer! *If you want to improve,* you must use your board and pieces. Set up every position on the board, and move the pieces about, as indicated in the explanatory comment. It is not enough to glance at a diagram hastily, murmur, "Of course, quite simple," and turn to the next situation. *Remember that physically playing out these combinations will help you to absorb and apply the basic combinative ideas in your own games.*

Two, and perhaps three, sessions should be devoted to the mastery of any single theme. The outline of every winning pattern, no matter how cleverly it may be disguised, will then become clear in any setting. You will learn by doing; when you have covered a theme in this thorough way, you will have a good grasp of its essentials. The quiz at the end of the section should prove quite easy.

A few words are in order about the chess notation. The moves actually played are given in bold face (*3* **B—K5**). Moves which might have been played (but weren't) are given in ordinary light face (*3* B—K5). It is a good idea to concentrate at the start on the moves actually played, turning later to the hypothetical alternatives. Note also the use of dots to indicate a move by Black. Thus, *3* **B—K5** tells us that White has played his Bishop to the fifth square in the King file; *3* . . . **B—K5** tells us that *Black* has played his Bishop to the fifth square in the King file.

In chess, we have an amazingly quick way of indicating good and bad moves, and the gradations in between. An exclamation mark (*3* **B—K5!**) tells us that the move is brilliant, perhaps the only way to win. Two exclamation marks (*3* **B—K5!!**) indicate an exceptionally fine move.

Just as the exclamation mark conveys our admiring and respectful attitude toward inspiration, the question mark is the typographical *tsk-tsk* which surrounds a bad move with an appropriate atmosphere of gloom and regret. Thus, *3* **B—K5?** is a mistake; *3* **B—K5??** is a catastrophic blunder.

Now for the gradations: *3* **B—K5!?** is a clever move which has unsound or risky features. The implication is that it may be ventured against an unwary opponent but not against a first-rate player. On the other hand, *3* **B—K5?!** is definitely unsound, but somewhat tricky. To sum up: *3* **B—K5?!** is a much weaker move than *3* **B—K5!?**

The study of the many examples and the methods of analyzing a combination should give you a better understanding of the combined powers of the pieces. The winning patterns will become familiar to you by their constant repetition. You will know when the scene is set for utilizing a double attack or a Knight fork or any of the other tactical devices discussed in the following pages. You will find that familiarity with the winning patterns gives order to unorganized chess thinking. The proper handling of the weapons of chess makes combination-planning second nature; and the use of combination play is the key to *Winning Chess*.

IRVING CHERNEV
FRED REINFELD

December 10, 1947

WINNING CHESS

1: FROM GOOGOLS TO TACTICS

Chess is as much a mystery as women—PURDY
Chess is 99% tactics—TEICHMANN

🐴THE TOTAL NUMBER of possible moves in a game of chess is staggering. The number is so huge that a googol * is quite trifling in comparison. Despite the googols of possible variations, chess is a fairly easy game. How is this paradox to be resolved?

The answer lies in Pascal's famous phrase: man is only a reed, but he is a thinking reed. Careful, systematic reflection about the game shows that all but a very minute proportion of the *possible* moves are *meaningless*: meaningless in the light of playing chess with a *purpose*. In chess, that purpose can only take the form of checkmating your opponent's King, or of preventing your opponent from checkmating your own King.

To play purposefully, therefore, we must discard the googols of possible moves and confine ourselves to only a microscopically tiny minority of all the possible moves.

Once we adopt this attitude of selectivity, we want to play only purposeful moves. Such moves have traditionally been divided into two broad categories: strategical and tactical. Some of the greatest authorities on the game have observed that tactics comprises 90% (if not more) of chess; *yet no chess book has been written in full recognition of this vital point.* The present volume is the first systematic

---

* We owe this charming term to Kasner and Newman's brilliant *Mathematics and the Imagination* (Simon and Schuster, 1940). They define the googol as 1 followed by 100 zeros.

treatment of tactics as the all-important, ever-present factor in winning chess.

Basically, all tactics may be reduced to these two methods:

1 Double attack

2 Concentration of superior force

Bidding a reluctant farewell to the googol, we shall now proceed to learn about these winning methods.

$\mathcal{2}$: WINNING WAYS

Tactics is the most important element in the middle-game—
TARRASCH
*No middle-game combination—however complex it may be—
can be anything more than a network of elementary smites
and compound smites*—PURDY

LET US BE CLEAR about what we mean by tactics.

Tactics is attack.

Tactics is the use of force—"smites"—smashing moves.

Tactics, then, is the imposition of your will on the enemy.

These statements tell us when tactics can be successful. Your attack must be stronger than your opponent's defense. You cannot impose your will on the enemy (checkmate his King or win material) unless you muster *superior* force.

On the previous page, we learned that there are two basic tactical methods. How do we apply them?

To execute the basic attacking ideas, we require *moves of violence*—forcible moves—forcing moves. All of them fall into one of the following groups:

1 A check and/or a capture

2 A threat to check and/or capture

The virtue of these violent moves is that they *cut down* the opponent's choice of a reply. It is this brusque elimination of choice which enables the attacking player to be exact in his calculations. It is this "imposing your will on your opponent" that sweeps away the googols of possible replies to any given move, leaving a minimum of responses to be reckoned with.

4

Of all the many thrills which chess holds for its devotees, none is perhaps so satisfying as the excitement that accompanies an attacking combination.

BASIC PATTERNS FOR TACTICAL PLAY

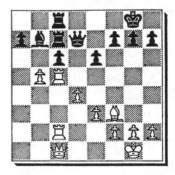

White checks the Black King, *and at the same time* he attacks Black's Rook. The King must move out of check, the Rook is captured next move. This is an example of *double attack*.

White attacks the weak Queen's Bishop Pawn *five* times; it is defended only *four* times. The Pawn cannot be saved. This is an example of *concentration of superior force*.

3: A SPADE IS A SPADE IS A SPADE

'*Twas brillig, and the slithy toves*
Did gyre and gimble in the wabe;
All mimsy were the borogoves,
And the mome raths outgrabe.
"*It seems very pretty,*" *she said when she had finished it,* "*but it's rather hard to understand!*" (*You see, she didn't like to confess, even to herself, that she couldn't make it out at all.*) "*Somehow it seems to fill my head with ideas—only I don't exactly know what they are!*"—LEWIS CARROLL

NOT SO LONG AGO, a New York plumber observed that hydrochloric acid was highly effective for opening clogged drain pipes. He enthusiastically passed on his discovery to the United States Bureau of Standards, which informed him, accurately but stiffly, that "The efficiency of hydrochloric acid is indisputable, but the corrosive residue is incompatible with metallic permanence."

When it developed that the plumber took this rebuff for high praise, a second warning was sent to him: "We cannot assume responsibility for the production of toxic and noxious residue with hydrochloric acid and suggest you use an alternative procedure."

The plumber remained obtuse and again thanked the Bureau. At this stage, another scientist was called in. His solution: "Don't use hydrochloric acid. It eats hell out of the pipes." *This* message was understood.

Many a chess book has suffered from similarly inflated verbiage. Franklin K. Young produced several volumes of such sonorous abracadabra as: "White's object is to form the *en potence* at once and afterward to establish the grand left oblique, while the minor crochet covers the right wing

5

against the adverse major front echelon" or "The minor left oblique refused is inferior to all strategic fronts directed either by the right or by the left or by the right refused."

In the present volume, an effort has been made to profit from the shortcomings of earlier books. In order to determine the relative importance of different types of attacking motifs, the authors examined thousands of games and tabulated the frequency with which the attacking themes occurred. From this they learned conclusively, for instance, that the pin unquestionably crops up more often than any other attacking method. It is therefore illustrated with the largest number of examples.

The terms for attacking themes have been selected with great care. In many cases they are self-explanatory (double attack, Knight fork, etc.). Each theme is described, reduced to a basic pattern, illustrated by practical examples, and then turned over to the reader in quiz problems.

One of the most serious faults in treating tactics is the custom of selecting examples of a given theme without isolating that theme from other, complicating, themes. Thus, the student may be shown a combination under the subject of Knight forks. It may also contain a double attack, a skewer, a discovered check, etc., etc.

In *Winning Chess,* the attacking themes are taught in cumulative fashion. The examples of pins concentrate on pins. The next chapter, on forks, includes pins but not more advanced subjects. In this way the reader's knowledge is widened gradually and systematically. Occasionally it has been found necessary to "jump ahead" to a more advanced theme; but such instances are rare.

A final word as to the quiz problems. They are easy— intentionally so; and solving them will give the reader that sense of power which comes from the execution of even the simplest chess combination.

4. THE PIN

The defensive power of a pinned piece is only imaginary—
NIMZOVICH
*The pin is mightier than the sword—*REINFELD

THE PIN is an attack against two or more hostile forces *standing on a straight line* (file, rank or diagonal). It is the most common, the most dangerous and hence the most important tactical weapon in the whole arsenal of combinations.

What makes the pin so potent is that the pinned piece is helpless and cannot move. The most vulnerable target of all is the one that is *immobile*. In chess, you may, and in fact you must, hit a man when he's down! Since the pinned piece is paralyzed, you pile up pressure on it, you exploit its powerlessness, you force a decisive gain of material.

BASIC PATTERN FOR THE PIN

1. **Black moves.** The Rook has just pinned the Bishop, which is *immobile;* it cannot expose the King to check. The Bishop cannot be guarded. The Rook will capture it next move.

2. **White moves.** He can win the exchange with *1* BxR*ch*. Instead, he exploits the Rook's helpless state: he *hits it again* with *1* **P—K3,** winning a whole Rook.

7

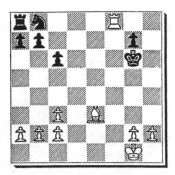

3A. White moves. He has taken advantage of the vulnerable position of the two Black pieces placed in a straight line. How? His Rook pins the Black Knight, which must not move because of the resulting loss of Black's Rook. How can White increase the pressure in order to exploit Black's predicament? The indicated answer is: *attack the Knight again!* Therefore: *1 B—B4!* See Diagram 3B.

4A. White moves. He is threatened with *1 . . . Q—B7 mate,* and there seems to be no way of saving the game. Casting about desperately for some resource, he notes that Black's King and Queen are placed *on the same straight line,* but that a Black Pawn blocks any chance of a pin by R—Kt1. Therefore, he removes the Pawn: *1 RxPch!!* See Diagram 4B.

5A. Black moves. With White's King and Queen diagonally in line, Black sees in a flash that if he can get his Bishop to B4, he will pin and win the Queen. But how is this possible, with White's Knight on Kt3 guarding the crucial square? This defender must be driven off!

| 1 . . . . | P—R5! |
| 2 Kt—Q2 | B—B4 |

See Diagram 5B.

3B. **Black moves.** His Knight is now menaced by two pieces, defended by only one. The *Knight is lost,* and will be captured by White on the following move.

In this example, we have seen how the pin functions in a *straight-line attack,* and how the pressure on a pinned piece is *intensified.* This is an important tactical device.

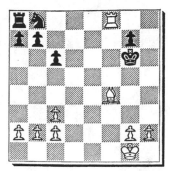

4B. **Black moves.** He can capture the violently sacrificed Rook by *1 . . . KxR* or *1 . . . QxR.* Whichever way he captures, his King and Queen *will be in a straight line.* Then comes *2 R—Kt1* pinning the Queen. In this way, White not only stops the mate, but actually wins the game. Defeat has been transformed into victory. *A pinned piece is a paralyzed piece!*

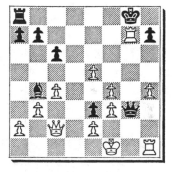

5B. **White moves.** His Knight's retreat surrendered control of the all-important pinning square B4. Now White's Queen is pinned and must be lost, with only a Bishop for scrawny compensation.

(Note: at move 2, White can move his King or Queen off the fatal diagonal. In that case *2 . . . PxKt* gives Black a winning material advantage.)

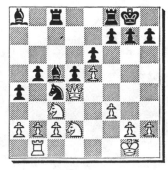

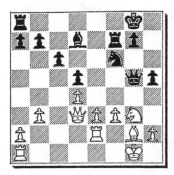

6A. **Black moves.** Here there are no less than three enemy pieces *on a straight line.* In such cases, the screening pieces (here the Knight and Bishop) are especially vulnerable to the advance of a hostile Pawn. Accordingly Black advances:

| 1 . . . . | P—R5 |
| 2 Kt—B1 | P—R6 |

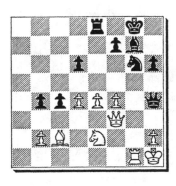

7A. **White moves.** This time it is Black who has two pieces between his King and the hostile potential pinning piece (the Rook). By this time, we know how to clear the path for the Rook's deadly pressure to be felt:

| 1 P—B5 | Kt—B1 |
| 2 P—B6 | . . . . |

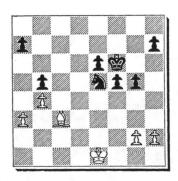

8A. **White moves.** The Knight is pinned in a particularly troublesome way; he is protected *only* by his King. When his Pawn moves are exhausted, the King will have to move, leaving the Knight unguarded. White begins with *1 P—Kt3*, and Black answers *1 . . . P—B5* intending to free himself from the pin with . . . K—B4. Now comes *2 P—Kt4!*

6B. **White moves.** White's Bishop is attacked, but, *being pinned, it is powerless to retreat* and will be captured by Black's King Rook Pawn. Note that (1) the lowly Pawn can be extremely dangerous when it advances to attack a pinned piece; (2) White can now block the line of attack with *3* **Kt—Kt3**—too late to save the Bishop!

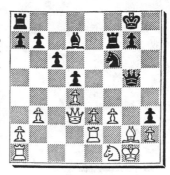

7B. **Black moves.** The Knight has been driven off, and his colleague, the Bishop, *is pinned.* Black must lose this piece: the attempt to free the Bishop by *2 . . .* **QxBP** fails after *3* **QxQ,** the Bishop being unable to recapture. With this defense knocked out, Black is helpless. *A pinned piece is a paralyzed piece.*

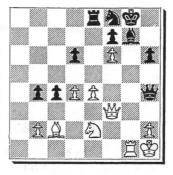

8B. **Black moves.** He must now resort to Pawn moves, as . . . K—B4 has been prevented. (Meanwhile White simply moves his King and Bishop to and fro—*a freedom not possessed by Black.*)

As soon as Black's Pawn moves run out, he will have to move his King, leaving the Knight unguarded. *A King is poor protection for a pinned piece.*

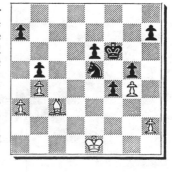

9A. Black moves. He exploits a pin *by concentrating on an overburdened piece,* in this case the White Queen. This piece has the *double duty* of protecting White's Rook and guarding against the convergence of Black's forces against KKt2. Black turns this to account:

1	QxPch!
2 QxQ	RxR

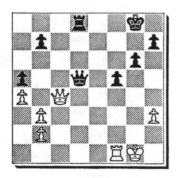

10A. White moves. His opponent threatens to *break the pin* with 1 . . . QxQ, remaining a Pawn ahead with a won ending. Therefore White must immediately make use of the pin: *"Hit him again while he's down."*

1 R—Q1!	QxQ
2 RxRch	. . . .

11A. White moves. His Queen is pinned and therefore *immobile;* but his Rook and Bishop are free to act. He can force Black's King and Queen onto *the same diagonal,* allowing a deadly pin. How?

1 R—R7ch	K—K1
2 B—Kt5	

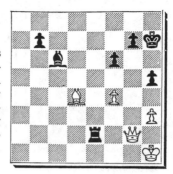

9B. White moves. His Queen is pinned by the hostile Bishop and attacked by the Rook as well. *3* QxR is clearly impossible *("a pinned piece is a paralyzed piece"!).* There is nothing left but *3* **QxB, PxQ,** leaving Black with the exchange and two Pawns ahead: an easy win for him. 10A runs on similar lines.

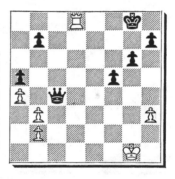

10B. Black moves. Instead of recapturing the Queen (which would have been a gross blunder), White took the Rook *with check!* Black must of course get out of check before doing anything else, whereupon White replies *3* **PxQ.** White benefits by the principle of *"Priority of check"*—a useful device.

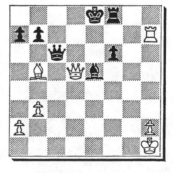

11B. Black moves. Although White's Queen is unprotected, *it is quite safe!* For Black cannot play 2 . . . QxQ*ch,* as that would expose his own King to check. (The typical quandary of the pinned piece!) Thus White wins the Queen and the game at once.

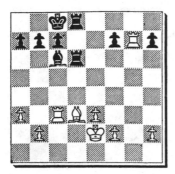

12A. **Black moves.** Effective pins can often be brought about *by replacing one hostile piece with another one on the same square.* In this case, the presence of Black's Rooks on the Queen file allows him to replace White's Bishop with a Rook, followed by a brutal pin with . . . B—Kt4:

| 1 . . . . | RxB! |
| 2 RxR | B—Kt4 |

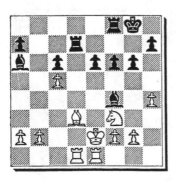

13A. **Black moves.** Again, in a very similar situation, Black sacrifices the exchange to bring about a pin:

1	RxB!
2 RxR	R—Q1
3 R—Q1	. . . .

Now Black's problem is *to apply more pressure immediately*—else White will release himself with 4 Kt —K1 and 5 K—B3. How does Black proceed?

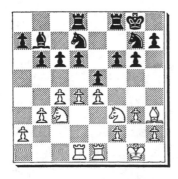

14A. **White moves.** It is by no means easy to discern prospects of a pin here; the intended target, Black's King Pawn, is defended three times and only attacked twice. White begins *by knocking out one of the defenders:*

| 1 BxKt! | RxB |
| 2 PxP | BPxP |

12B. **White moves.** Behold! His opponent's sacrifice of the exchange has produced a position in which White's King and Rook *occupy the same diagonal.* They are thus vulnerable to a Bishop pin which is absolutely decisive; for White can offer the wretched Rook no further support, and the piece is irretrievably lost.

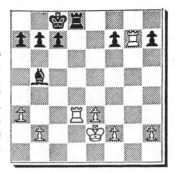

13B. **Black moves.** His King, Rook and Bishop at KB5 can do nothing to strengthen the pin. By elimination, we arrive at the Pawns. There lies our solution! Black plays *3 . . .* **P—K4!,** and White is helpless against *4 . . .* **P—K5** winning the Rook. Once more we see the value of the maxim *"Hit him again while he's down!"* Note how these basic themes recur.

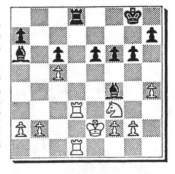

14B. **White moves.** And now the point: *3* **KtxP!** Black's Queen Pawn is pinned, for *3 . . .* PxKt allows *4* RxR. Note that White's clever first move brought Black's Rook to a square (Q2) *where it was no longer guarded by its fellow Rook.* Let us see more examples of how players are forced into pins.

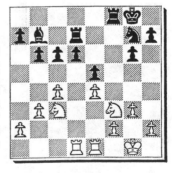

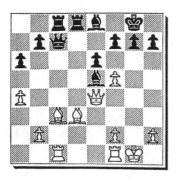

15A. Black moves. Again and again we shall stress the importance of picturing to oneself the consequences of *every possible check or capture.* A check gives the opponent no alternative to getting out of check; a capture almost always calls for instant recapture. *The opponent's lack of choice makes calculation easy:*

1	BxP*ch*
2 K—R1	B—B3

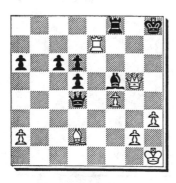

16A. White moves. The presence of Black's King and Queen *on the same open diagonal* makes us sense the possibility of a winning pin. Obviously, *1* B—B3 is pointless, as Black simply removes the unguarded Bishop. How, then, do we proceed from intuition to analysis? We call on the White Queen for assistance:

1 Q—R4*ch*	K—Kt1
2 Q—Kt3*ch*	K—R1

17A. White moves. Black is badly pinned right at the start, with his King, Queen and Bishop on the same rank with White's Rook. Yet Black's position is well barricaded, and it does not seem easy to exploit the Bishop's unfortunate position. But **a simple capture works wonders:**

1 RxR!	PxR
2 P—K6!	....

15B. White moves. The check *forced* White's King onto a white square. Then, with both King and Queen *on the same diagonal,* the pin with *2 . . .* B—B3 naturally proved deadly. Had White played *2* K—Kt2, the result would have been the same; in each case he loses Queen for Bishop. In 16A, we shall need to find two checks before we force their Majesties into a fatal pin.

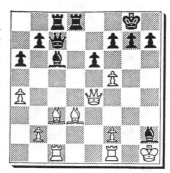

16B. White moves. Nothing has been changed but the position of the White Queen. But what a big "but!" For now the White Queen *protects the square QB3,* making possible the crushing sequel *3* B—B3, winning the hostile Queen. The zig-zag checking maneuver, so innocent in appearance, changed a potential pin into a winning pin. Now let us see how *captures* may prove useful.

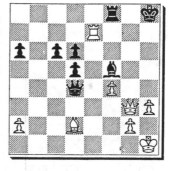

17B. Black moves. He must lose a piece, for after *2 . . .* QxQ (it is clear that *2 . . .* BxP would be disastrous); *3* KtxQ *the pin still functions,* and Black must lose a piece!

Note the ease with which this can be worked out: we know that if we play *1* RxR!, Black must retake; thus the road is cleared for the King Pawn's successful advance.

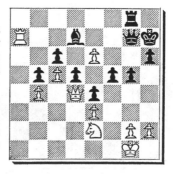

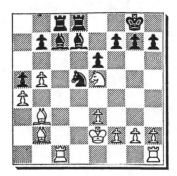

18A. White moves. Again, capturing technique sets the stage for a devastating pin. White sees that after he plays KtxB and Black retakes, the remaining Bishop will be pinned, the Rook on the last rank unprotected. In that event, 2 P—Kt6 would be decisive . . . if only Black did not have the resource of 2 . . . KtxKtP. The proper procedure is:

1 KtxB	RxKt
2 BxKt!	RxB

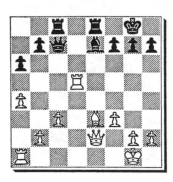

19A. Black moves. He uses the little trick of first exchanging, and then pinning the recapturing piece. Play begins with *1 . . .* **B—B4!** White guards the pinned Bishop with *2* **R— Q3** (if *2* RxB, QxR; *3* BxQ, RxQ and Black has won the exchange).

Now Black *changes the pinned piece* (as in 12A and 13A, page 14) by *2 . . .* **RxB!** White replies *3* **RxR.** What has Black gained?

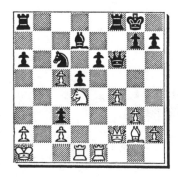

20A. White moves. Bearing in mind that captures limit the range of his opponent's replies, White dabbles with the possibility of *1* KtxP! The point is that after the obvious reply *1 . . .* **BxKt,** White continues with *2* **RxB!**—all part of his plan. Let us now take stock of the situation in Diagram 20B.

18B. White moves. The removal of the Knight has cleared away the final obstacle to the execution of White's plan: we are left with a simple pinning position on the Queen Bishop file. One more blow at Black's paralyzed Bishop is needed: *3 P—Kt6* wins a piece. Once more the maxim of *"hit him again while he's down"* has proved its usefulness. In 19A we get another example of the same technique.

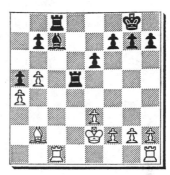

19B. Black moves. He has given up the exchange in order to replace White's Bishop on K3 with White's Rook. *"Hitting him again while he's down,"* Black puts on more pressure with *3 . . . R—K1.* To the inexperienced player, this move is startling— Black's Rook is unprotected. But of course this Rook cannot be captured, for *"a pinned piece is a paralyzed piece."* Black now wins a Rook.

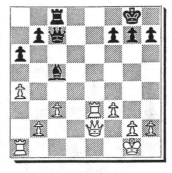

20B. Black moves. To his horror, Black discovers that if he plays *2 . . . QxR,* he has put his King and Queen *diagonally in line,* so that *3 BxP* produces a pin which wins the Queen!

If Black retreats his Queen, there follows *3 RxKt.* White wins another Pawn with easy victory in sight.

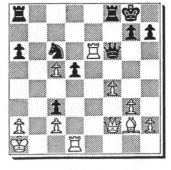

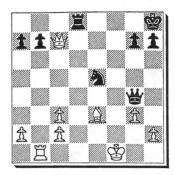

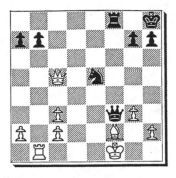

21A. **Black moves.** He begins with the aggressive *1 . . . Q—B6ch,* forcing *2 B—B2* (why?). Now that the Bishop is pinned, Black increases the pressure by *2 . . . R—KB1,* threatening mate. White must defend with *3 Q—B5.*

21B. **Black moves.** Now another—and final—blow at the helpless Bishop: *3 . . . Kt—Kt5* wins the piece, as White cannot bring up any more defensive forces. A splendid example of how to "pile up" on a pinned piece.

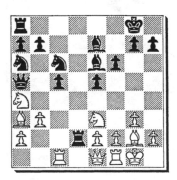

22A. **White moves.** The target here is Black's awkwardly placed Rook at Q7. First we force Black into a real pin by removing his Queen's protection: *1 BxKt!* Black must reply *1 . . . PxB;* but now his Queen is unguarded and the Rook is really pinned!

22B. **White moves.** Now that the target is immobile, we *"pile up"* on it: *2 R—Q1.* Black defends with *2 . . . R(R1)—Q1.* So far, so good. But we continue to "pile up" on the wretched Rook: *3 B—B1.* Black has no more defensive resources and suffers decisive loss of material.

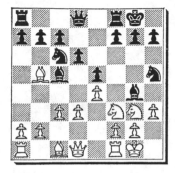

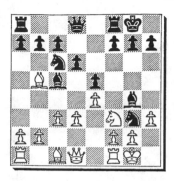

23A. **Black moves.** When a player castles King-side, his King's Bishop Pawn is often pinned by the hostile King Bishop. In this case, White is trying to drive off the hostile pinning Bishop. He has overlooked Black's reply, which wins the exchange: *1 . . . KtxKt!*

23B. **White moves.** His Rook is attacked by Black's Knight. The reply 2 PxKt is impossible because White's King Bishop Pawn is *pinned*. White must therefore play **2 PxB**, permitting the loss of the exchange by 2 **. . . KtxR.** *A pinned Pawn is a paralyzed Pawn!*

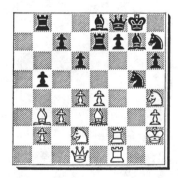

24A. **White moves.** Observe how his opponent's pieces are all jumbled together. His Queen, normally the strongest piece on the board, *has no move whatever!* *1* **Kt—Kt6!** exploits this tragicomic situation.

24B. **Black moves.** What a predicament! His Queen is lost. As in 23A, his King's Bishop Pawn is *pinned* and cannot capture the interloper. But here the stakes are much higher. A fantastic finish.

QUIZ ON PINS

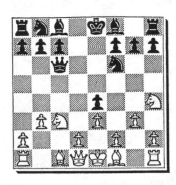

25. Black moves. *Mindful of the axiom "the defensive power of a pinned Pawn is only imaginary," how does he win material at once?*

26. White moves. Black's King and Queen are *diagonally in line. What winning idea does White immediately look for?*

27. White moves. *Is there a direct pin? If not, can he exchange and then enforce a winning pin?*

28. White moves. *How can he force Black's King and Knight into a pin? How will White then add pressure to the pin?*

(Solutions for Diagrams 25–30 are on page 227)

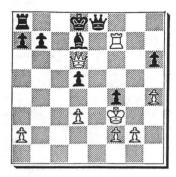

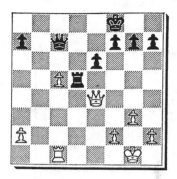

29. White moves. Black's King and Queen *are in line. Is there a winning pin?*

30. Black moves. *Is 1 . . . Rx P advisable?* If not, give your objection to it.

BREAKING A PIN

Whenever a new weapon of warfare was discovered in the "good old days," someone soon found an antidote. When battleships were first constructed with armor that could withstand any shell, inventors immediately set to work to perfect a shell that could pierce any armor.

As in war, so in chess. Despite the enormous power of the pin, there are times when its pressure can be broken. Occasionally one can slip out of a pin with Houdini-like slickness; *but more often, a pin must be broken by violent measures.* These may take the form of a check, a mating threat, a counter-pin, counterattack, capture or undermining the pinning piece.

Remembering these terms is unnecessary: the important thing is to seek the *violent* move—to meet force with more force. This insistence on violence is logical enough; to break a pin, *you have to apply more force than is originally exerted by the pin itself.* For examples of this process, see pages 24–28.

31A. White moves. He sees that his opponent's King and Queen *are in line* on the King file; therefore he plays *1* **R—K1** pinning the Black Queen. Despite the fact that the Rook is guarded by White's Queen, this move is a gross blunder. This Black demonstrates by breaking the pin, which must be done *at once*: *1 . . .* **BxP***ch.*

32A. Black moves. He apparently has no way to save his badly pinned Knight. If he is to break the pin at all, it must be by *brute force. 1 . . .* Kt—K6 is unsatisfactory, for after *2* BxQ, KtxQ; *3* QRxKt White has won a piece.

But Black has a remarkable resource at his command: *1 . . .* **KtxB!!** White naturally replies *2* **BxQ**.

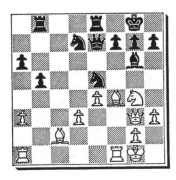

33A. White moves. Black's Knight at K4 is pinned: moving it would cost Black the exchange. White wants to strike at the pinned Knight (already attacked three times!) still another time. As a rule, the most effective way to do this is to *hit the pinned piece with a Pawn*, therefore: *1* **P—Q4**. Instead of meekly losing the exchange, Black, showing great presence of mind, replies *1 . . .* **R(Kt1)—B1!!**

31B. White moves. His only means of getting out of check is to move his King. If *2 K—Kt2, BxRch* wins at once: it removes the pinning piece and also wins White's Queen. If *2 K—R1, QxRch* again removing the pinning piece and remaining with an enormous material advantage. White's pin was tempting but much too superficial.

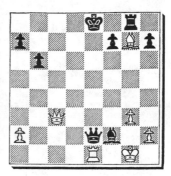

32B. Black moves. Why did Black give up his Queen? He has three pieces trained on the White King, two of them converging on the vital King Knight Pawn. His next move ends all argument: *2 . . . BxP* mate!

In this sensational example, Black saved himself with a mate threat; in 31A a check was sufficient.

33B. White moves. White's quadruple attack on the pinned Knight has been ably parried by his opponent's counter-thrust. If White captures the pinned Knight, Black simply answers *2 . . . RxB.*

White therefore decides on *2 B—Kt3,* which is answered by *2 . . . KtxKt.* The pin is broken, and Black has satisfactorily extricated himself from his difficulties.

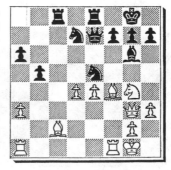

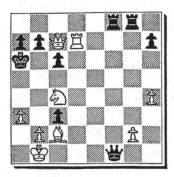

34A. White moves. Black is giving check *and simultaneously attacking the Knight.* White is helpless to salvage the Knight, but he notes that after it is captured, *Black's King and Queen will be diagonally in line.* A pin by B—Q3 will then be feasible. So:

1 R—Q1	QxKt
2 B—Q3	. . . .

35A. Black moves. How can he increase his pressure on the pinned Bishop? Not by *1 . . .* R(R1)—KB1, even though the Bishop is then attacked three times and defended twice. This would be useless, for *2 . . .* QxB would obviously be out of the question. Black therefore strikes at the Bishop *with a Pawn*—the best way: *1 . . .* P—KKt4. White tries his only defense: *2* Q—Kt4, pinning the pinner!

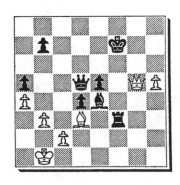

36A. White moves. He is a Rook down but sees a ray of hope. Black's King and Queen are in direct line, permitting the pin *1* B—B4. Black cannot immediately remove the Bishop, which is supported by a Pawn. But this Pawn is in turn *supported by a Pawn which is pinned!* Hence the Knight's Pawn is not really protected!

34B. Black moves. A desperate situation, but he does not lose hope! He plays *2 . . . P—B7ch!* White must now choose between *3 BxP* (upon which the pin disappears) or *3 K—B1,* when *3 . . . PxR(Q)ch* dramatically *removes the Bishop's defender!*

The resourcefulness of Black's surprising tactics is quite striking.

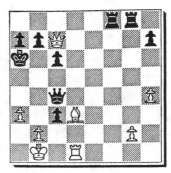

35B. Black moves. If he moves his King to B1 (not *2 . . . K—R1??; 3 B—K5* with a winning pin) to unpin the King Knight Pawn, White has time to retreat his Bishop. Hence, if Black is to break the pin, he must do so at once. The way to do this is *2 . . . P—KR4!* White's Queen *must release the pin,* allowing Black to win the unfortunate Bishop.

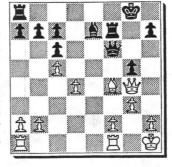

36B. Black moves. He plays *1 . . . RxPch!* removing the Bishop's *false support.* White answers *2 BxR* (*2 Px R* is impossible, and other moves allow *2 . . . QxB*). The Queen is still pinned, but now comes *2 . . . Qx Bch* removing the pinning piece. White cannot capture, as his Bishop's Pawn is *pinned!*

QUIZ ON BREAKING A PIN

37. Black moves. White has just played P—B4, hitting out at the pinned Bishop. *How does Black break the pin, winning at once by demonstrating that the advance of the Pawn was a mistake?*

38. Black moves. His Knight is attacked twice, defended only once and cannot obtain any additional support. *Yet Black can release himself from the pin by creating a mating threat with . . . ?*

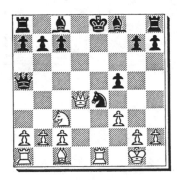

39. Black moves. White's last move was P—B3, striking at the pinned Knight. *What counter-pin will give Black a decisive advantage?*

40. Black moves. His Knight is badly pinned. *What violent counterattack breaks the pin and saves the game for him?*

(Solutions on page 227)

5: THE KNIGHT FORK

He was a verray parfit gentil knight.
But for to tellen yow of his array,
His hors were gode, but he was nat gay—CHAUCER
The Knight, as it were, mocks the rest of the men by pass-
ing under or over them!—ZNOSKO-BOROVSKY

THE KNIGHT is the showman of the chessboard. Perhaps our fondness for this picturesque figure is a nostalgic reminder of the days when knighthood was still in flower and man's noblest friend was the horse and not the tin lizzie. Equally striking is the Knight's *move*, the delight of the mathematician and the terror of the chess novice. It is with the insidious but elegant Knight fork that this piece reaches the height of its effectiveness.

The fork is a simultaneous attack on two or more hostile forces. In contrast to the bludgeon-like blows of the other pieces, this thrust is suggestive of the rapier.

BASIC PATTERN FOR THE KNIGHT FORK

41. **White moves.** Black's Knight has moved from Q4 to K6, attacking three pieces: White's Queen and both Rooks. The threats are as deadly as they are graceful: *a Knight attack does not permit interposition to ward off the blow.* Knight forks occur almost as often as pins; it is vital to recognize forking opportunities as they arise. Expert handling of the Knights is the hallmark of a fine player.

29

42A. White moves. He has a Knight fork at his disposal, although it seems futile to look for it when his Knight is *pinned* and unable to move! To find the combination (and nearly all of chess is analysis of combinations), *we must examine every possible check or capture.* Then we can anticipate the following:

1 QxKt*ch!*   QxQ
2 Kt—B5*ch*   . . . .

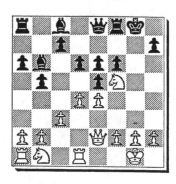

43A. White moves. Here the Knight fork is brought about *by forcing the hostile King and Queen into a vulnerable position.* This is just as important as looking for a pin when the enemy's pieces are on the same straight line.

White plays *1* **Q—Kt4*ch*,** realizing that *1* . . . K—R1 or *1* . . . K—B2 is impossible because of *2* Q—Kt7 mate. Therefore *1* . . . Q—Kt3 is forced, allowing *2* Kt—K7*ch*.

44A. White moves. He sees that he has a murderous check at K7— if only Black's Bishop did not guard this forking square. He therefore *removes the protective Bishop*:

1 **KtxB**   **PxKt**

(Forced: the Queen has no flight square.)

2 **Kt—K7*ch***   . . . .

42B. **Black moves.** White's surprising Queen sacrifice set the stage for the elegant Knight fork which followed. This violent thrust *unpinned* the Knight, freeing it for the fork pictured above. The deadliness and economy of the fork on King and Queen displays this tactical device in its most attractive form. In the following example, a mating threat is used to produce the same effect.

43B. **Black moves.** His King and Queen were in position for the *coup de grace.* As we have seen, the fatal fork could not be prevented because of the mate threat.

In these first two examples, White was able to force the forking combination by means of capture or mate threat. In the next example, capturing is again employed, this time to remove a piece which momentarily prevents a fork.

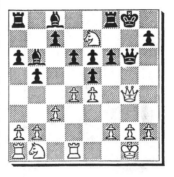

44B. **Black moves.** Having removed the hindrance to his plans, White was able to execute an elegant Knight fork. Black must move his King, allowing the Knight to capture the Queen.

Note the way in which the Knight *simultaneously* strikes in two directions! We continue with captures which lead to Knight forks.

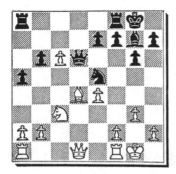

45A. Black moves. When you plan a combination, *you must review every possible check and capture.* Black sees that *1* . . . Kt—B6*ch* would win White's Bishop if the forking square were not protected by White's Queen. Yet there is a way to lure the Queen from the protection of KB3: *1* . . . QxB!! This is pretty much the same combination as in 42A.

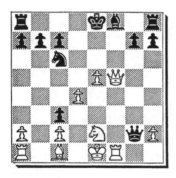

46A. Black moves. He is a Pawn ahead, but his King is exposed to attack. He frees himself from all difficulties with the astonishing resource *1* . . . QxKt*ch!* Thereby he gives up the Queen for only a Knight; but after *2* KxQ we see the point: *2* . . . KtxP*ch.*

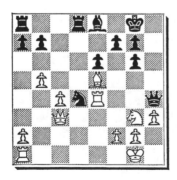

47A. Black moves. He is just on the point of losing a piece, as his Queen and Knight are simultaneously attacked. (In fact, his Knight is attacked no less than three times!) Can Black extricate himself? Yes:

1	QxR!!
2 KtxQ	Kt—K7*ch*

The Knight fork attacks King and Queen; the pattern is becoming familiar!

45B. White moves. He naturally replies 2 QxQ. Has Black made a mistake? No; he has simply followed *the basic combinative principle of examining every possible capture and check on the board.* Now comes 2 . . . Kt—B6*ch,* a pretty forking move which regains the Queen and leaves Black a piece ahead. Such opportunities are frequently overlooked.

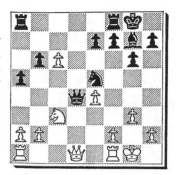

46B. White moves. The fork works its usual magic: King and Queen are attacked. After 3 K—Q3, KtxQ; 4 RxKt the transaction winds up with Black another Pawn to the good.

In this case, *the fork was utilized as a means to a favorable simplifying exchange* on Black's part.

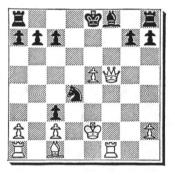

47B. White moves. His King must get out of check, whereupon Black replies 3 . . . KtxQ, coming out the exchange ahead.

Note how Black carried through the Knight fork idea at K7, *even though his opponent guarded the square with two pieces at the outset. 1 . . . QxR!!* removed one of the protective pieces; when White's Knight captured the Queen, the other guard disappeared.

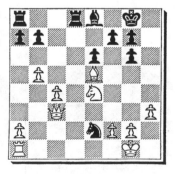

48A. **White moves.** The only forcing measure is a check: *1 R—R8ch*. Black must interpose: *1 . . . B—Q1.* Now there is a win by *2 Kt—B6* followed by a general exchange of pieces. But something even more *forceful* is available.

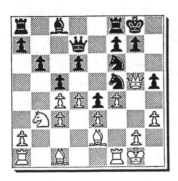

49A. **Black moves.** The scope of the White Queen is severely limited. This prompts Black's first move; the object is to drive the Queen to an even more unfavorable square, when Black is sure to profit thereby.

| 1 . . . . | Kt—R2 |
| 2 QxP | . . . . |

50A. **White moves.** His extra Pawn is not enough to assure an easy win. Following our rules, he looks for *a check or capture. 1 KtxPch* is not feasible, as the Queen Bishop Pawn is *doubly protected*. But, continuing to look for *violent moves*, we hit on this:

| 1 R(R4)xKt! | RxR |

48B. White moves. Our rule for planning combinations still holds: *examine every capture and check!* Therefore: 2 **RxB***ch!* (a capture *and* a check), **KxR** and now the pretty Knight fork 3 **Kt—B7***ch* wins the Rook.

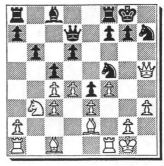

49B. Black moves. White's last move was forced. Now Black's other Knight leaps in at Kt6, attacking Queen, Rook and Bishop, and forcing the win of the exchange.

When a hostile piece (in this case the White Queen) *has little mobility, it is often vulnerable to attack.*

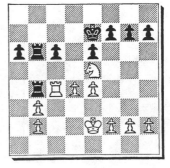

50B. White moves. If he plays 2 KtxP*ch*, then 2 . . . RxKt leaves each player with a Rook apiece. Instead, White obeys an important general principle: *when you have a choice in capturing, take the most important enemy piece.* Thus: 2 **RxR!**, RxR and now the fork 3 **KtxP***ch* leaves White a piece ahead!

51A. White moves. He has a strong move here in *1* QR—K1 (pinning!). But he prefers a clearer, because more forceful move. White therefore plays *1* Kt—Q5, already picturing a piquant Knight fork in his mind's eye. Continuing to guard his exposed Knight, Black replies *1* . . . Q—K3.

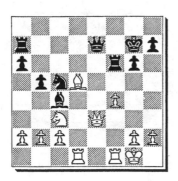

52A. White moves. You will recall that a pin is sometimes given decisive effect through the medium of *preliminary exchanges*. This is also true in the case of forks.

Here White begins by capturing Black's strongest piece, *which automatically indicates Black's reply.* This is an infallible basis for the play to come.

   1 QxQch   RxQ

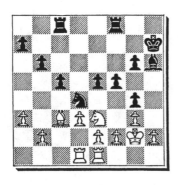

53A. Black moves. He begins with *1* . . . BxKt! in order to force a pretty Knight fork. White would like to play *2* BxKt to eliminate the dangerous Knight, but this would lose a piece (why?). White therefore plays *2* PxB. Black replies *2* . . . Kt—B7!, revealing his nefarious little plan.

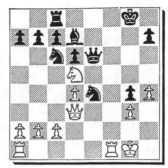

51B. White moves. Now White sacrifices his Queen! He plays *2 Qx Kt!* Startling? Yes, but not surprising if you are familiar with *the principle of examining every possible capture.*

The continuation was *2 . . . QxQ; 3 Kt—B6ch*—winning by a particularly pleasing Knight fork.

52B. White moves. After the previous exchange, it is easy to see that the Black Rooks would be particularly susceptible to a Knight fork at Q5. How can we vacate this square for *immediate* occupation by the Knight? By another exchange, of course!

    2 BxB   *PxB*
    3 Kt—Q5   . . . .

The Knight fork wins the exchange.

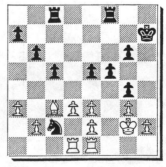

53B. White moves. Wherever he moves the menaced Rook, there follows *3 . . . KtxPch,* forking King and Rook. The sequence is enchantingly economical: (1) Black removes the protective Knight; (2) he gains time by attacking a Rook; (3) he wins the other Rook by a forking check, with the exchange to the good.

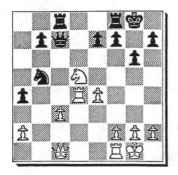

54A. **Black moves.** His Queen is attacked by White's Knight. Should the Queen flee timidly?—or should we apply the rule of first *looking at every possible check or capture?* Several captures are possible, and one of them is good; but which one is it? The move is *1 . . . KtxR!* And there is method in its madness!

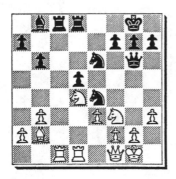

55A. **White moves.** He begins with *1 Kt—B6,* attacking the Rook at Black's Q1. Relatively best is *1 . . . RxKt,* losing "only" the exchange. But suppose Black is stubborn and tries to save the Rook? Then we get *1 . . . R—K1; 2 Kt—K7ch!* with a "family check" on Black's King, Queen and Rook! A remarkable concentration of force.

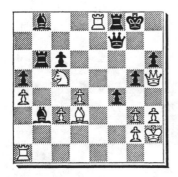

56A. **White moves.** He winds up cleverly with *1 QxQch, KxQ (1 . . . BxQ* leads to the same result); *2 Rx Rch, KxR; 3 Kt—Q7ch* and the Knight fork menaces King *and* Rook.

Follow the discussion of this position under 56B to grasp the principle illustrated here.

54B. White moves. He naturally plays *2 KtxQ.* Then comes the expected Knight fork *2 . . . Kt—K7ch,* and after *3 K—R1, KtxQ* Black is a whole Rook to the good.

On his first move, Black applied the same principle as in 50B: If you have a choice of captures, *take the most important enemy piece.*

55B. Black moves. He *must* capture the Knight, as the Queen is attacked. There follows *2 . . . RxKt* allowing *3 RxRch* followed by *4 RxB* (after *3 . . . Kt—B1*). Thus the family check has made it possible for White to win a whole Rook. *The fork was a preliminary to attack on the last rank.*

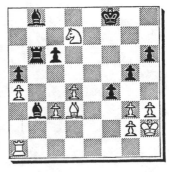

56B. Black moves. After he removes his King from check, he will lose his Rook—a hopeless situation.

As in 52A, we have seen something instructive: *how a series of even exchanges, which in themselves involve no gain of material, can lead to such gain.*

57A. White moves. Again we apply the stratagem of *a series of exchanges,* but here the play is tricky. We begin with *1* BxP!, BxB*ch* (can you see how *1* . . . PxB loses the exchange?); *2* RxB!, PxR; *3* RxR, RxR. White is a Rook down. What has he accomplished? But here is the point: *4* Kt—K7*ch!*

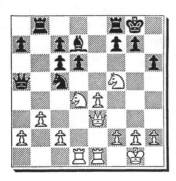

58A. White moves. The winning idea is forceful, pleasing and startling. White begins with the Knight fork *1* KtxBP!—a surprising move since Black replies *1* . . . BxKt(B3). But now comes *2* Kt—K7*ch,* forking King and Bishop. Black's King goes to R1.

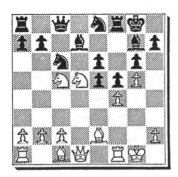

59A. White moves. He begins with a surprising move: *1* Kt—Kt6!, a Knight fork which menaces Queen, Rook and Bishop. Black naturally plays *1* . . . PxKt and White counters with *2* KtxB. What has White accomplished so far? He now has *two* threats.

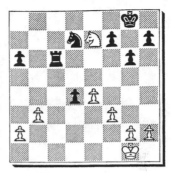

57B. **Black moves.** Now everything becomes clear. The Knight check, forking King and Rook, regains the lost material and leaves White a Pawn ahead with an easily won ending.

So we see that *the previous exchanges were only a means to an end*: a preparation for the eventual fork.

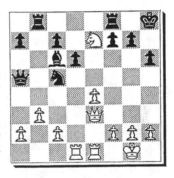

58B. **White moves.** He continues with *3 KtxB*, ending up with the exchange to the good.

Black was able to parry the first fork, but this turned out to be *preliminary* to the second *and* third forks, which could not be parried!

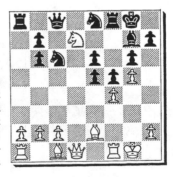

59B. **Black moves.** He plays *2 . . . R—B2*, as the Rook was attacked. But *3 KtxKtP* forks Queen and Rook and wins the exchange. Observe that the *violent* character of *1 Kt—Kt6!* enabled White to foresee the consequences, *since Black had no choice.*

BREAKING A KNIGHT FORK

He acts most wisely who makes his plans with caution, recognizing that any untoward event may occur—HERODOTUS

What has been said about freeing oneself from a pin (page 23) applies in large measure to the methods of breaking a Knight fork. In either case the break must be accomplished as a rule by a *violent* move: elimination of the threatening piece; counterattack; capture; check; threat of mate.

Two examples should suffice to illustrate the point:

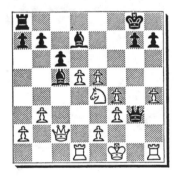
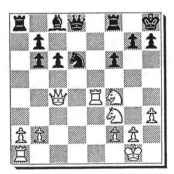

60. **Black moves.** His Queen and Bishop are menaced by a Knight fork. He breaks the attack by *1 . . . B—R6ch; 2 RxB* (forced), **Q—Kt8** mate. Black saved himself by means of a *violent move,* in this case a check.

61. **White moves.** He refutes the Knight fork by means of an unexpected mating attack: *1 Kt —Kt6ch!,* **PxKt** (again forced); *2 R—R4* mate. In this instance, also, the attack was nullified by a *violent move*: a sacrificial check.

We come now to a study of the two attacking methods, the pin and the fork, in combination. Together, they make a fearsome weapon—one which can be admired and enjoyed, and must be mastered!

THE FORK AND THE PIN

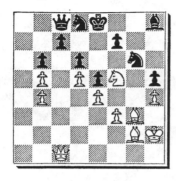

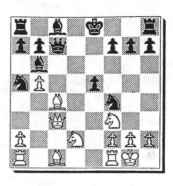

62. **White moves.** He wins by combining *the fork and the pin*: *1* **KtxPch** forks King and Queen. If Black replies *1 . . .* **PxKt**, then *2* **QxQ.** Thus he loses his Queen *through a fork or a pin.*

63. **Black moves.** He plays *1 . . .* **Kt—K7**ch forking the King and Queen. True, White can play *2* **BxKt**, but then comes *2 . . .* **QxQ.** *The pinned Bishop cannot parry the forking check.*

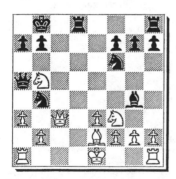

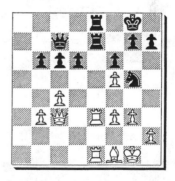

64. **Black moves.** He continues *1 . . .* **Kt—B7**ch*,* forking King and Rook. White's Queen is *pinned,* therefore helpless to prevent the fork. After *2* **K—B1** there follows *2 . . .* **QxQ** and *3 . . .* **KtxR.**

65. **Black moves.** *1 . . .* **KtxP** ch forks King and Rook at K1. *2* **RxKt** must be played, allowing the loss of the exchange by *2 . . .* **RxR.** White's Rook at K3 was *pinned;* therefore its protection of the Pawn was an *illusion.*

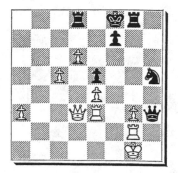

66A. Black moves. He begins with the most violent move on the board: a capturing check. His opponent's reply is forced. Thus the consequences are easy to foresee:

1	QxRch!
2 KxQ	Kt—B5ch

The point!

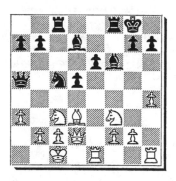

67A. Black moves. It is not easy to see at first glance that a pin can arise in this position. Exploiting the fact that his Queen Rook and White's King are in line, Black plays 1 . . . P—Q5 and White retreats 2 Kt—K2 (other Knight moves are no better). Now the villain appears: 2 . . . Kt—Kt6ch.

68A. Black moves. His target is the King's Bishop Pawn—although it is defended by three pieces! He begins with a capture, 1 . . . KtxB, enabling him to foresee White's reply, 2 QxKt. Now the vulnerable point has only two defenders—*one of them pinned!* But how does the Knight fork materialize?!

66B. White moves. The delightful Knight fork (based on a pin) will leave Black a Rook ahead after White's King moves and Black replies 3 . . . KtxQ. The fact that White's Knight Pawn is *pinned* in the above diagram is what makes the combination possible.

67B. White moves. He is helpless: the Knight forks his King and Queen, and the White Queen Bishop Pawn, *being pinned,* is unable to capture the intruder! *"A pinned piece is a paralyzed piece."* So White must move his King, allowing his Queen to be captured. A subtle example of this theme.

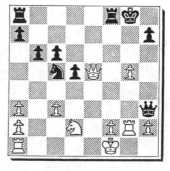

68B. Black moves. He strikes at once: a *violent* move is required, before the defense can be reinforced. The solution: 2 . . . RxPch! As White's Rook is pinned, he is limited to 3 KxR (allowing 3 . . . Kt—Q6ch); or 3 K—K1 (again allowing 3 . . . Kt—Q6ch); or 3 K—Kt1 (allowing 3 . . . QxR mate). *The fork and pin* worked hand in glove!

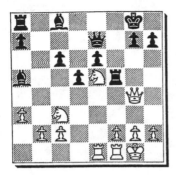

69A. White moves. He wins by a neat combination involving two successive Knight forks followed by a capture based on a pin. In actual play, this is easier done than said! White begins with *1 KtxBP,* a Knight fork threatening Queen and Bishop. This forces *1 . . . Q—QB2,* and now comes the astonishing fork *2 Kt—K7ch* attacking King and Rook.

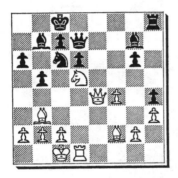

70A. White moves. White utilizes a Knight fork, not to gain material, *but as a means to an end*—to enforce a pin. He begins with *1 Kt—Kt6ch,* attacking King and Queen. Black must therefore reply *1 . . . PxKt.* Now the point: *2 B—K6.*

71A. White moves. *1 RxB!* is indicated: he sacrifices the exchange for *a lasting pin.* Black must reply *1 . . . RxR,* when *2 R—KB1* adds to the pressure. Black defends with *2 . . . R—KB1* (only one Rook can go to this square—which Rook?). Now *3 Q—Kt5* again adds to the pressure. Black will be unable to withstand the hammering on his pinned Rook.

69B. Black moves. He plays 2 . . . QxKt (else 3 KtxR winning the exchange). Now comes 3 QxR! with a simple and familiar pinning position. Whether White succumbs to 3 . . . PxQ; 4 RxQ or not, he is the exchange down. Picture 69A *without the Knight at K5,* and the capture QxR immediately strikes your eye. *White forced this position with no loss of time.*

70B. Black moves. His Queen is pinned, and must be lost. (The attempt to break the pin with 2 . . . R —K1 is foiled by 2 BxQ*ch*—remember *the priority of check!*) White's *forceful* first move left Black no choice; it also *cleared the path* for the Bishop.

71B. Black moves. He brings up his last reserve to defend the beleaguered Rook: 3 . . . K—Kt2. Now comes a stunning *coup de grâce:* 4 Kt—R5*ch!* The Knight fork attacks the Rook a fourth time, exploits the Bishop's pinned position as well (*the Bishop cannot capture*) and smashes the defense against the pin. The King must move: the Rook is lost. Bravo!

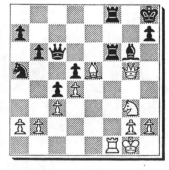

QUIZ ON KNIGHT FORKS

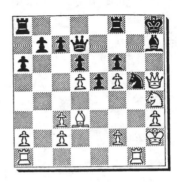

72. White moves. *How does he sacrifice his Queen in order to win with a Knight fork?*

73. White moves. *How does he take advantage of a pin in order to win material with a Knight fork?*

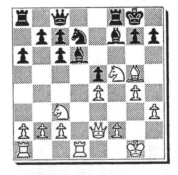

74. White moves. *How does he win a piece at once? How does a threatened Knight fork prevent Black from regaining his piece?*

75. White moves. *What does White play in order to create the possibility of a devastating Knight fork at K7?*

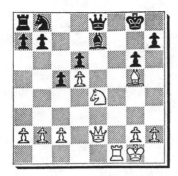

76. **White moves.** *How does he profit by a pin in order to gain decisive material by a Knight fork?*

77. **White moves.** *What violent first move will lead to a winning Knight fork the second move?*

(Solutions for Diagrams 72–77 are on pages 227–228)

6 : DOUBLE ATTACK

All combinations are based on a double attack—FINE
Examine moves that smite!—PURDY
The advantage of attacking two men at once is evident in that
probably only one of them can be saved—EDWARD LASKER
It is a mistake to think that combination is solely a question of
talent, and that it cannot be acquired—RETI

IN EVERY GAME or sport, there are certain feats that connote mastery. The perfect dive, the clever bridge finesse, the precisely executed forward pass, the swift and deadly double play, the superb lift of the pole vault—these and many others thrill us with their perfection.

In chess, we get the same reaction from the *double attack*. Such a stratagem, symbolizing the triumph of mind over matter, is of the very essence of the game. The master of the double attack stamps himself as an expert: by skilful manipulation of his forces, he renders two hostile units helpless by means of a double attack *with only one of his own units*. What a sense of power such wizardry confers!

As we know from what we have read so far, *double attacks will be most effective when based on forceful, violent moves*. It will therefore come as no surprise to us that the following double attacks operate by means of mating threats, checks, attacks on loose pieces, irresistible Pawn pushes, pins and the like. In a game of chess, there must be no rest for the weary!

DOUBLE ATTACKS WITH MATING THREATS

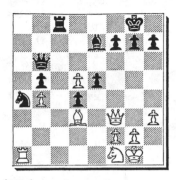

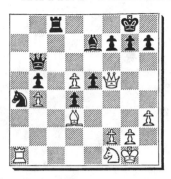

78A. White moves. Double attacks need not necessarily be directed against two pieces. The type of attack which menaces a piece *while threatening mate* is often deadly and certainly difficult to ward off. White *plays 1 Q—B5* with a *double threat.*

78B. Black moves. His Rook is menaced by the Queen, and at the same time *2 QxRPch, K— B1; 3 Q—R8 mate* is threatened. *The combined threats* are too much for Black. He must stop mate, losing his Rook in the process.

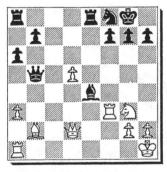

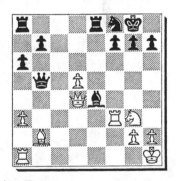

79A. White moves. He is under a double attack, as both his Rook at KB3 and his Queen's Pawn are attacked. *1 Q—Q4!* threatens mate and *simultaneously* attacks the Bishop a second time.

79B. Black moves. He must defend the mating threat with *1 . . . P—B3*, leaving his Bishop in the lurch. Then comes *2 KtxB, RxKt; 3 QxR, QxB; 4 R—K1* and White has won the exchange.

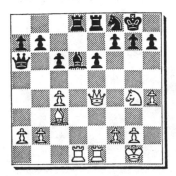

80A. White moves. Here a double attack must be *created!* 1 Q—Q4 (threatening mate) would not do because of *1 . . .* B—R7*ch* (discovered attack!) winning the White Queen. In any event, there would be no real threat after *1* Q—Q4: Black would stop the mate, after which *2* QxB would be too expensive (the Bishop is protected by a Rook). All very complicated, but the solution is deliciously simple:

    1 RxB!   RxR

81A. Black moves. He operates with two *double attacks* to achieve his objective. First comes *1 . . .* Q—K2, attacking White's Rook and also threatening *2 . . .* Q—K8 mate. White parries by defending his Rook and at the same time providing an outlet for his King: *2* P—KR4. Is White safe now?!

82A. Black moves. He plays to win the Pawn at his K5, as it is protected twice, while he attacks it three times. His calculations are mathematically correct; yet he loses because he overlooks the eventual *double attack.*

1	KtxP?
2 BxKt	RxB
3 RxR	QxR

80B. **White moves.** His sacrifice of the exchange has forced Black's recapturing Rook into a really exposed position. *Such loose pieces make wonderful targets for a double attack.* Hence the logical sequel readily suggests itself: *2 Q—K5,* with designs on the unguarded Rook in addition to the mate threat on KKt7. Black must stop this mate. While he does so, he loses the hapless Rook.

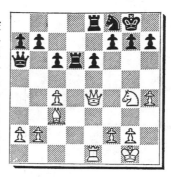

81B. **Black moves.** No indeed, White is not safe: *2 . . . Q—K8ch; 3 K—R2* and now we have a second double attack: *3 . . . QxPch* winning the Rook. Although this combination is four moves long, it is easy to execute; *the double attacks are so forcing that they dictate White's replies.*

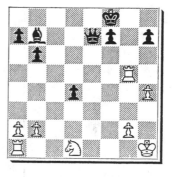

82B. **White moves.** This is as far as Black has calculated, and he appears to have done well; for now White's Knight is attacked. But a Knight at KB5 is always aggressively posted, and a double attack is in the cards: *4 Q—Kt5!* This threatens mate and also attacks the loose Rook at Q8. The double attack wins at once for White.

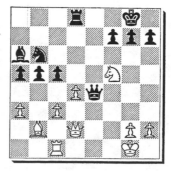

DOUBLE ATTACKS WITH CHECK

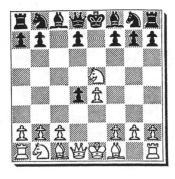

83A. Black moves. His target is the unprotected Knight at K5. If he attacks it by some such move as *1 . . . P—Q3*, the Knight can simply retreat and nothing has been accomplished. But if Black can threaten the Knight *and some more important object simultaneously*, the Knight will be lost! The right way is *1 . . . Q—R4ch!*

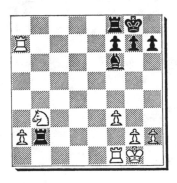

84A. Black moves. He sees in a flash the *potential* double attack *. . . B—Q5ch*. Unfortunately, White's Knight guards the important square and thus prevents the killing check. What can Black do about the Knight? Answer: *he can remove it!*

1	RxKt!
2 PxR	. . . .

Now Black's plan is feasible.

85A. White moves. Who would dream that he has a double attack at his disposal?! The method is the familiar one of *substitution*: he replaces the Black Bishop on QKt5 with another Black piece—one that is *vulnerable to double attack*. A little sleight of hand does it:

1 RxB!	RxR

Now this Rook is on the same line with the Black King.

83B. White moves. He must get out of check before doing anything else! He has seven ways of getting out of check, *but none of them can save the Knight.* Black's next move will be 2 . . . QxKt.

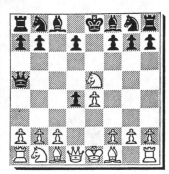

An important illustration of the use of a check to win material which the opponent is not given time to defend!

84B. Black moves. White had to accept the sacrifice of the exchange. Now the path has been cleared for 2 . . . **B—Q5***ch.* Black wins the exposed Rook, coming out a piece to the good. The whole transaction may seem startling, but it was rigorously logical. Black had a plan; saw a hindrance; then disposed of the hindrance in the most forcible way: *capture!*

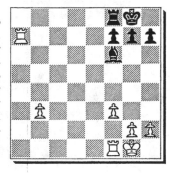

85B. White moves. Taking advantage of the position of the hostile King and Rook, White plays 2 **B— B5***ch* winning the Rook and coming out a piece ahead.

It is a useful habit, and one that facilitates analysis, to picture the *immediate consequence of every possible capture.* Well-protected squares and pieces often lose their defenders through such captures.

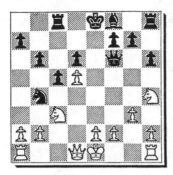

86A. White moves. As in 80A, it is possible to *create* a target for double attack. Here the method is to force a hostile piece to a square *on which it will be unprotected*. White begins with *1 P—QR3*, attacking the Knight. Such Pawn pushes cannot be disregarded, as they threaten a decisive gain of material (winning a piece for a Pawn). *1 . . . Kt—R3 is* therefore necessary.

87A. White moves. Black's Rook is defended by the Bishop, but the Bishop in turn *has no defender.* He can be attacked in various ways, but the most economical is by way of a *check.* Hence White maneuvers the Black King into position for a double attack: *1 Q—R8ch.*

88A. White moves. As in the case of other attacking motifs, the process of forcing a series of *preliminary exchanges* will often wind up in a *double attack.* Frequently the final capturing piece is left unguarded; a position that seemed impregnable suddenly gives way.

1 BxB	KtxB
2 RxKt!	RxR

86B. **White moves.** Black's Knight has *been forced into position for a double attack*. White plays *2* **Q—R4ch** and picks up the Knight after Black's King has moved out of check.

Note that the check is only *a means to an end* in these examples: the check is secondary to the objective of gobbling up the other enemy piece which is under attack.

87B. **Black moves.** He has only one way of getting out of check, by playing *1* ... **K—Kt4.** Now the King and Bishop are in line for a double attack. White plays *2* **Q—K5ch** (or *2* **Q—Q8ch**), winning the Bishop. Again the check has been a means to an end.

88B. **White moves.** He has given up the exchange in order to force the Black Rook to a square where it is *unprotected*. Is there a check which will take advantage of the Rook's vulnerable state? *3* **Q—Kt5ch** is the move. Black must attend to his King's safety, leaving the defenseless Rook to its fate. The Bishop on R3 *had to be replaced by the helpless Rook*.

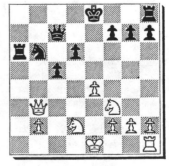

89A. White moves. To bring about the desired position, we require *a series of preliminary exchanges*:

1 **RxB!**	**RxR**
2 **RxR**	**QxR**

89B. White moves. He has succeeded in stripping the Rook of its defenders. *3* **Q—Kt4***ch* now wins the Rook in familiar fashion. Such combinations occur frequently in practical play.

90A. White moves. *1* **P—Kt5!** clears the diagonal for the White Queen. *1 . . .* **PxP** is forced, as the Rook at KB3 must remain at its station to guard the Knight. Now the first point: *2* **RxKt!** (stripping the Rook at QKt2 of its defender), **RxR;** *3* **RxR, Qx R.** What now?

90B. White moves. The stage is set for the double attack: *4* **Q—B8***ch* wins the unprotected Rook! A number of factors have coalesced: the doubled Rooks are strong; the White Queen wants to get into play; Black's Rooks are vulnerable. A very pleasing example of this theme.

DOUBLE ATTACKS ON LOOSE PIECES

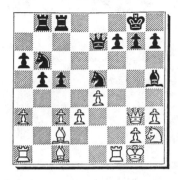

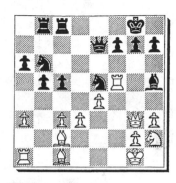

91A. White moves. *Unprotected pieces* (like Black's Bishop here) *are the best possible targets for double attack.* 1 **R—B5** menaces the Bishop, and the Knight at K4 as well.

91B. Black moves. His Knight is now attacked by two pieces, defended by only one. After *1 . . . B—Kt3* (what else is there?) White captures the Knight, winning a piece.

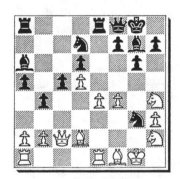

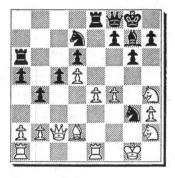

92A. White moves. Black's Knight at Kt6 is an *exposed piece,* but it can always save itself by the forceful move (*capture!*) . . . KtxB. White kills this resource by *1 BxB,* forcing *1 . . . RxB.* Now White is ready for the *double attack.*

92B. White moves. Black's forced recapture has made it easy for White to foresee the next step. The Knight at Kt6 is now really exposed, and in addition the Rook at R3 has become a *loose piece.* White wins a piece with *2 Q—Q3!*

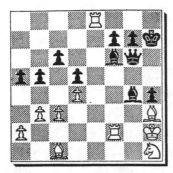

93A. Black moves. His object is to penetrate with his Queen into the enemy's territory. Black begins with *1 . . . BxB*, and after *2 KxB* he is ready to carry out his plan: he makes good use of the Queen's attacking potentialities.

93B. Black moves. The previous exchange has drawn White's King away from the protection of his Knight. Now both White's Knight and Bishop are *exposed pieces*. *2 . . . Q—KKt8* threatens both pieces and wins one of them.

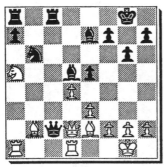

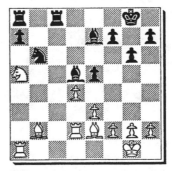

94A. Black moves. Picture this diagram with the Queens removed. In that event, both White Bishops would be *loose pieces,* vulnerable to the double attack . . . R—B7. How can Black force this ideal situation?

```
1 . . . .               QxQ
2 RxQ                   . . . .
```

94B. Black moves. *White's Rook must be driven off!* Then his Bishops will be undefended. The logical move is *2 . . . B—Kt5.* To avoid losing the exchange, White must play *3 R(Q2)—Q1.* This permits *3 . . . R—B7,* winning one of the Bishops (the visualized position!).

DOUBLE ATTACKS WITH THE PAWN PUSH

95A. **Black moves.** He employs a double attack to prepare for a second double attack—a witty idea. First comes *1 . . . P —Q6*, attacking Queen and Knight and forcing *2 RxP*. To this the reply is *2 . . . RxR!* forcing *3 QxR.* Why did Black give up a Pawn?

95B. **Black moves.** Now the second, and this time fatal, double attack: *3 . . . P—K5*, menacing Queen and Knight. He can try to break the double attack by *4 BxKt*. But Black warily replies *4 . . . PxB!* and the double attack remains, forcing the win of a piece.

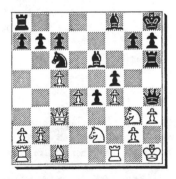

96A. **White moves.** He plays *1 P—Q5*, a double attack which wins material *indirectly.* The Bishop and Knight are attacked, so that *1 . . . BxQP* is forced.

96B. **White moves.** He continues with *2 KtxBP*, a Knight fork attacking Queen and Rook. So the initial double attack was not an end in itself!

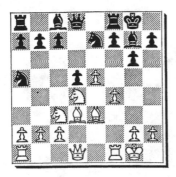

97A. Black moves. An attack by a piece on a piece of equal value can be met in various ways. For example, you can defend the threatened piece so that its capture will result in an even exchange. Not so with attacks by *Pawns*: the threatened piece must flee at once. (To support it and permit its capture by a Pawn would mean losing a piece for only a Pawn.) Black plays *1 . . .* **P—QB4.**

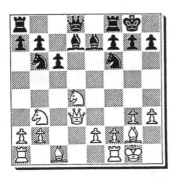

98A. Black moves. Another Pawn push *to gain time* for the subsequent double attack by a Pawn: *1 . . .* **P—B4** attacks the Knight at Q4. White has no choice: he must retreat the Knight at once; no other move can be considered. The Pawn attack admits of no alternative to retreat. There follows *2* **Kt—B3,** and now comes the Pawn fork *2 . . .* **P—B5** (the second half of the Pawn push).

99A. White moves. He hits the Knight at K3 with *1* **P—Q5.** As we know, the Pawn push forces the threatened piece to run away; bringing up a defender is of no avail, as it would only lose a piece for a Pawn. Black plays *1 . . .* **Kt—B2**—the only square left for the attacked Knight. Now for the second part of the Pawn push: *2* **P—Q6.**

97B. **White moves.** As we know, the Knight cannot remain under attack. He must retreat! There follows: *2 Kt—B3,* and now comes the Pawn fork *2 . . . P—Q5.* The double attack by the Pawn wins a piece.

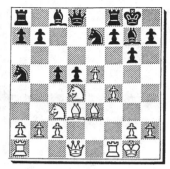

This example gives an impressive idea of the power of the Pawn push. It is a frequent means of winning material, as *it severely cuts down the opponent's choice of defensive replies.*

98B. **White moves.** His Queen and Knight are attacked by the on-rushing Pawn. *The more important* of the two menaced pieces, the Queen, must be saved, allowing *3 . . . PxKt* with a piece to the good for Black.

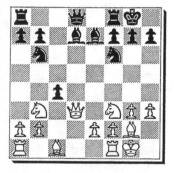

White was helpless to ward off the double attack, as Black's first Pawn push *left no time for defense* against the second Pawn advance. *The choice of reply was severely restricted.*

99B. **Black moves.** The Knight retreated to his only available square, but this did not save him from a devastating Pawn fork. (In 98A, the Pawn fork was effective because the Pawn was guarded by a Black Knight; here the forking Pawn is protected by the Bishop.) As only one of the Knights can be saved, Black is forced to lose a piece.

DOUBLE ATTACKS WITH PINS

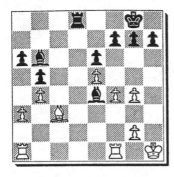

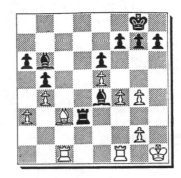

100A. Black moves. An interesting form of double attack is one directed against a piece and a square already weakened by a pin. Black begins with the *forcing* 1 . . . R—Q6. White defends with 2 QR—B1.

100B. Black moves. The two-edged nature of his previous move is brought out by the sequel: *2 . . . R—R6 mate!* The White Pawn is pinned, and *the defensive power of a pinned piece is only imaginary!*

101A. White moves. He operates with a double attack against King and Queen.

1 KtxBch	PxKt
2 Q—Kt4ch	K—R1
3 Q—R4	K—Kt2

101B. White moves. Relying on the fact that a pinned piece is paralyzed, White exploits the pin by *4 Q—Kt5ch!* The King is driven off to R1, whereupon *5 BxPch* wins the Queen as scheduled.

BREAKING A DOUBLE ATTACK

As in the case of the pin and the fork, the defender's thrust for freedom must generally be of a *violent* nature: a mating threat, a check, a capture, a counterattack, etc. Some examples, by no means exhaustive:

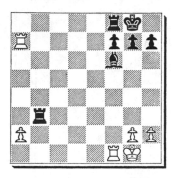

102. **White moves.** (adapted from 83A) He nullifies both threats by interposing: *1 B—B3!*

103. **White moves.** (adapted from 84A) Instead of playing *1 PxR?* (allowing *1 . . . B—Q5ch*), he equalizes with *1 RxB!*

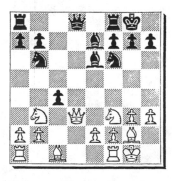

104. **White moves.** He frees himself from the double attack on Knight and Queen by means of *1 Q—Kt1ch!*

105. **White moves.** He escapes from the Pawn fork with *1 QxQ!* and then retreats his Knight, with no loss of material.

QUIZ ON DOUBLE ATTACKS

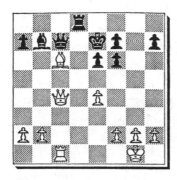

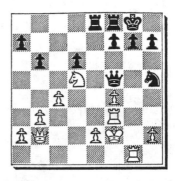

106. White moves. *How can White make use of a double attack with check to win a piece?*

107. White moves. *How does he win a piece at once by double attack on two loose pieces?*

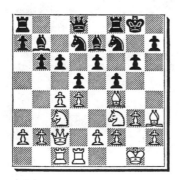

108. Black moves. *How does he take advantage of a two-move Pawn push to win a piece by double attack?*

109. White moves. *Find the double attack which wins a piece by attacking it and simultaneously threatening mate.*

(Solutions on page 228)

7: DISCOVERED ATTACK

*He who has imagination without learning, has wings and no feet—*JOUBERT
*Methodical thinking is of more use in chess than inspiration—*PURDY
*The combination player thinks forward; he starts from the given position, and tries the forceful moves in his mind—*EMANUEL LASKER

THE DISCOVERED ATTACK is a move involving two *distinct* and *simultaneous* thrusts at enemy units. As one piece moves, *checking or capturing or threatening*, it unmasks the action of another piece against the opponent. The diagram below illustrates this process drastically.

The destructive force of this attack is enormous: it is as though you were moving two pieces at the same time! As a rule, the simultaneous attack cannot be parried simultaneously; the defender must ignore the less important threat, bitter though his reluctant choice may be.

BASIC PATTERN FOR DISCOVERED ATTACK

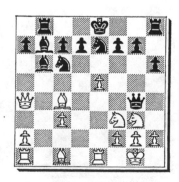

110. White moves. The position of the two Queens, with the Bishop between them, constitutes the *basic pattern*. The Bishop makes a *"discovered attack"* by *1 BxPch!* Black sees that his Queen is attacked, but he cannot save her, because of the rule of *priority of check*. White's next move will be 2 QxQ.

67

DISCOVERED ATTACK WITH CHECK

111A. White moves. He sees at once that the forces on the Queen Bishop file are arranged in the basic pattern for a discovered attack. *Any* move of White's Bishop will release his Rooks. A *check* or a *capture* (or a combination of both!) will keep Black too busy to save his Rook at QB1. So White plays *1* **BxPch!** This is surprising at first sight, for the Bishop can be captured in four different ways!

112A. Black moves. A vulnerable target must be *created* here. Black's Bishop at KB4 attacks the Queen's Pawn *directly*. Black's Rook at Q1 attacks it *indirectly*. Black's Bishop at Q3 can give check. Add up these three factors, and you have a combination! We start with *1 . . .* **BxP!** White must reply *2* **QxB,** unless he prefers to lose the exchange by running away with the Queen.

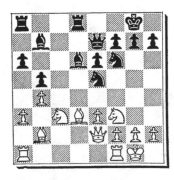

113A. Black moves. Our solution of 112A gives us a clue here: *we must unmask an attack on the Queen file.* We therefore begin with an exchange which will bring White's Queen into a vulnerable position for the discovered attack. We begin with *1 . . .* **KtxB,** forcing *2* **QxKt** (unless White prefers to remain a piece down). Now comes the discovered attack: *2 . . .* **BxPch!**

111B. Black moves. *He must get out of check at once.* If he plays *1 . . .* **RxB,** then *2* **RxR***ch* and White is the exchange ahead. Other moves by Black lead to the same result.

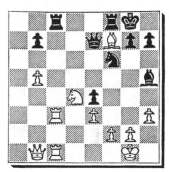

The fact that White gives check as he "discovers" on the *inadequately* guarded Rook is the key to the combination. Had this Rook had additional protection, the combination would have been impossible.

112B. Black moves. Now he has the position he wanted. He must "discover" an attack on the Queen *at once,* so that she cannot escape. Only one move will answer that requirement: *2 . . .* **BxP***ch* attacking the White King with the Bishop, *and* attacking the White Queen with the Rook! White must reply *3* **KtxB,** whereupon *3 . . .* **RxQ** wins. *Q.E.D.*

113B. White moves. *He must get out of check,* permitting the loss of his Queen by *3 . . .* **RxQ.** We are becoming familiar with the basic pattern for the discovered attack. The Black Bishop *masked* a possible attack on White's Queen. Therefore we moved the Bishop with check, *unmasking* the Rook's attack on White's helpless Queen. Remember the *priority of check!*

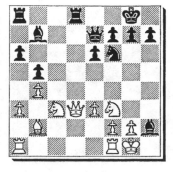

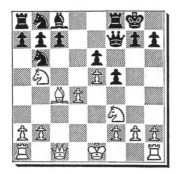

114A. White moves. One of the most dangerous features of the discovered attack is that it is often *a concealed weapon*. In the diagram, for example, White's Queen has enormous power on the Queen's Bishop file, even though its action is masked by the White Bishop. There follows *1 KtxBP!*, threatening to remove the Black Rook. Black naturally answers *1 . . . QxKt*.

115A. White moves. Here his problem is *the correct sequence of his moves*. There is a potential attack via the Queen file, but how is White's Bishop to leave Q4 in order to unmask an attack by the Rook? *1 BxQKtP??* is a gross blunder because of *1 . . . QxBch*. *1 BxPch, KxB; 2 RxKt* is much better, but wins only a Pawn. The correct sequence begins with *1 BxKt!*, which must be answered by *1 . . . QxB*.

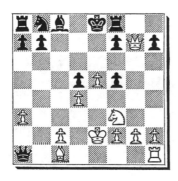

116A. White moves. He has just sacrificed a Rook, relying on the basic pattern for a discovered attack which is now available. The position on the first rank is suggestive: White's Bishop is obviously going to *unmask an attack on the Black Queen*. But how, with Black's King on a white square?! White cuts the Gordian knot: *1 QxRch!* Black replies *1 . . . KxQ*.

114B. White moves. He has the basic pattern for a discovered attack: *he can unmask an attack* on Black's Queen by giving check with his Bishop. Obviously the discovery must be engineered by the Bishop, which momentarily blocks the avenue of attack against the Black Queen.

The logical move is 2 **BxPch,** forcing the win of Black's Queen because of *the priority of check.*

115B. White moves. Black has been given no option. That is the first good point about the proper order of moves. The second valuable feature is that *the Black target has been transformed* from a Knight into the immensely valuable Queen. Now comes 2 **BxPch,** "discovering" a Rook attack on Black's Queen, which is lost next move. Also feasible is 2 **BxQKtP,** winning a piece by "discovery."

116B. White moves. Now that Black's King is on a black square, White continues 2 **B—R6ch** winning the Queen, as Black must get out of check. With a Pawn ahead, White wins easily. Suppose that after *1 QxRch,* Black had replied *1 . . . K— Q2. There would still be a "discovery" pattern* after 2 **Q—Q6ch, K—K1;** *3* **B—Kt5!** threatening mate!

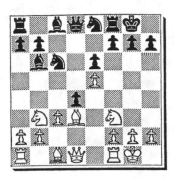

117A. White moves. This diagram illustrates a basic idea which occurs innumerable times. To understand and apply this idea, you need only understand the pattern for discovered attack: White's Queen is a *potential* threat to any piece on the Queen's file, *even though momentarily masked* by the Bishop.

1 PxP	KtxQP?
2 KKtxKt	BxKt
3 KtxB	QxKt

118A. Black moves. The possibility of a discovered attack is obscured here; *but when you know the pattern, you know what to look for.* The decisive clue is the fact that White's Queen *is not protected.* Black begins with a Knight fork sacrifice: *1 . . .* Kt—B6*ch*. White's Rook is attacked, so he plays *2* PxKt. Now *2 . . .* Q—Kt3*ch* forces *3* K—R1. The pattern for a discovered attack is established!

119A. White moves. White's Bishop seems to have but little scope, yet it is easy to imagine a situation in which the Bishop attacks through the medium of a forceful utilization of the Knight. The problem is to make a *possible Knight check* practical. The doubled Rooks give us a point of departure:

1 RxKt!	KtxR
2 RxKt	QxR

117B. White moves. Now Black's *un*guarded Queen has become a vulnerable target. White *unmasks a discovered attack* with *4* **BxPch**, winning the Queen.

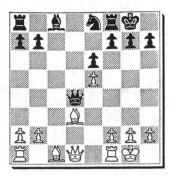

What makes this common combination even more valuable is that it often arises when the opponent's King is uncastled; in that case, the final move is B—Kt5*ch*. The details may differ; *the pattern is the same, and must be known!*

118B. Black moves. His Queen is now on the same diagonal as the adverse Queen—separated only by a Black Knight; *a perfect setting for a discovered attack.* Black plays *3 . . .* **Kt—Kt6***ch*, forcing White to do something about the check. Consequently White has no time to save his defenseless Queen. *Had White's Queen been protected,* the combination would have been impossible.

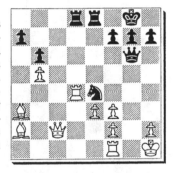

119B. White moves. The situation is cleared up, giving us a sharp focus on the Bishop's attacking possibilities: he is now *on the same line with the hostile Queen.* We need a Knight move which attacks a piece *even more important* than the Queen. *3* Kt—K7*ch* is refuted by *3 . . .* Qx Kt. Therefore the move we seek is *3* **Kt—R6***ch*, and now Black gets out of check only at the cost of losing his Queen.

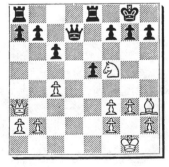

DISCOVERED ATTACK WITH CAPTURE

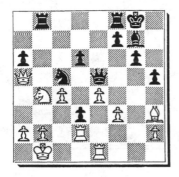

120A. Black moves. He sees a familiar *pattern* in the position of the two Queens, with the Knight between them. What move can the Knight make which will be a *"smite"* while at the same time exposing White's Queen to attack? Black has no check and no mate threat, but he does have a *capture:* 1 . . . KtxP!

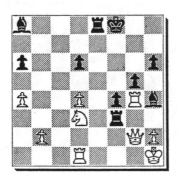

121A. Black moves. He produces a drastic example of the crushing power of the discovered attack. The key idea is to move his Rook from KB6, *unmasking an attack* by his Bishop on White's Queen. To create the most havoc, he combines this "discovery" with a *capture:* 1 . . . RxKt! Note that White's Queen is now pinned and cannot guard the Rook at Q1!

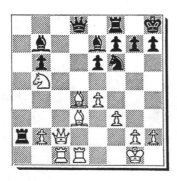

122A. White moves. Both his Bishops mask a possible attack by his Rook on Black's Queen. To bring about a discovered attack along the Queen's file, *it is necessary to move the Bishops.* First comes a *threat:* 1 B—B4, attacking Black's Rook on QR7. Black replies *1 . . . R—R1. Now we have gained time to devise the proper setting for the discovered attack.*

120B. White moves. He is in a terrible predicament! He cannot capture the Knight, for his Queen is *en prise*. Nor can he merely move his Queen out of the line of attack, for then 2 . . . KtxR*ch* will win both Rooks. White must submit to playing 2 QxQ, KtxR*ch!* (this *interpolation* is vital!) followed by 3 . . . BxQ.

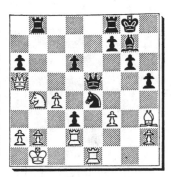

121B. White moves. He is threatened with 2 . . . RxR mate. If he plays 2 RxR, then comes 2 . . . R—K8 mate (remember the Queen is pinned!). White therefore tries 2 QxB, hoping for 2 . . . RxQ?; 3 RxR etc. But, utilizing the *priority of check* (as in 120B) Black plays 2 . . . RxR*ch!* first, confiscating White's Queen later on, and remaining a Rook and Bishop ahead.

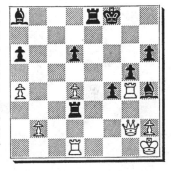

122B. White moves. He "discovers" an attack on Black's Queen by moving his Bishop from Q4. The most forceful Bishop move is a *capture*: 2 BxKt. This wins a piece, as Black must stop to save his Queen.

In 120A and 121A it was possible to "discover" an attack by immediate capture. Here the capture required a little preparation.

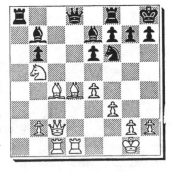

DISCOVERED ATTACK WITH SECONDARY THREAT

123A. Black moves. By moving his Bishop, he can uncover an attack on White's Knight. The Bishop cannot check, capture or threaten mate. What *forceful* possibility remains?! *He can attack!* Therefore: *1 . . .* **B—R6.** Black's Queen attacks the Knight; Black's Bishop attacks the Rook.

124A. Black moves. Even the "humble" Pawn can be the instrument for uncovering an attack, while it attacks a *different* piece.

1	**KtxKt**
2 QxKt	**P—Q4!**

This poisonous Pawn push was not easy to anticipate. At first sight, it seems quite meaningless; it takes a practiced eye to see the *secondary threat.*

125A. White moves. A discovered attack is indicated on the Queen's Bishop file. But there is a difficulty to be ironed out: White's Queen is *en prise!*

1 KtxKt	**RxKt**

White has killed the attack on his Queen and he has also created a *subsidiary target* for a discovered attack. How?!

123B. **White moves.** He must lose some material, as *both Knight and Rook are menaced.* His "best" course is to save his Knight, allowing the loss of the exchange.

If White tries 2 B—Kt2? (hoping for 2 . . . QxKt?; 3 BxB) there follows 2 . . . BxB! with a piece to the good.

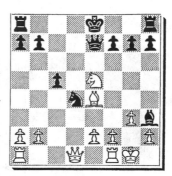

124B. **White moves.** By advancing, the Black Pawn has attacked the Queen, *simultaneously* opening up the diagonal of his King's Bishop for an attack on White's unguarded Bishop on QR3.

If this Bishop were *protected,* or if White's Queen could retreat and *support* the Bishop, the discovered attack would fail. But White lacks these defensive resources; hence he loses the Bishop.

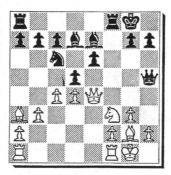

125B. **White moves.** He continues with the pretty move 2 Kt—Kt5, *discovering* attack on Black's Queen by the White Rook, and at the same time *forking* Black's Queen and Rook with the Knight. Black must move his Queen (obviously 2 . . . PxKt? is out of the question); and after 3 KtxR, White winds up the exchange ahead. *The double threat was too potent to be parried.*

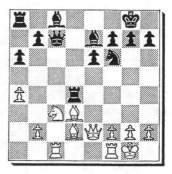

DISCOVERED ATTACK WITH MATE THREATS

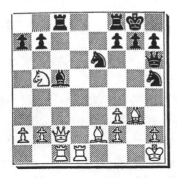

126A. Black moves. The position on the Queen's Bishop file calls for a discovered attack on White's Queen by a move of Black's Bishop.

    1 . . . .   KtxBch
    2 BPxKt   B—Kt8!

126B. White moves. Black has "discovered" an attack on White's Queen; at the same time the *unmasking* Bishop creates the terrible threat . . . QxP mate. White must lose at least a piece (*3* **B—B4, RxB**).

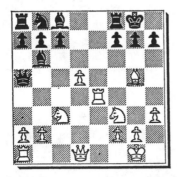

127A. White moves. He begins by driving the Black Rook at KB1 into position for the *discovered attack pattern*: *1* **B—K7**. Black replies *1* . . . **R—K1**. Now *2* **B—Kt4** threatens *3* RxR mate, or *3* BxQ.

127B. Black moves. He cannot move his Queen in such a way as to guard the *unprotected* Rook. Hence he must give up his Queen to stave off the mate. A particularly virulent example of discovered attack!

QUIZ ON DISCOVERED ATTACKS

128. White moves. *By what discovered attack does he win the Queen?*

129. White moves. *By what discovered attack does he win a piece?*

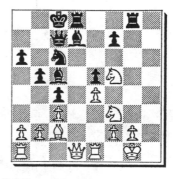

130. Black moves. *By what discovered attack does he win the Queen?*

131. Black moves. *By what discovered attack does he win a piece?*

(Solutions on page 228)

8: DISCOVERED CHECK

Discovered check is the dive-bomber of the chessboard—FINE
*Order and simplification are the first steps toward the mastery
of a subject—the actual enemy is the unknown*—THOMAS
MANN

DISCOVERED CHECK is an *intensified* and hence even more potent form of discovered attack. Each stratagem confers the advantage of simultaneously blasting two enemy forces. The stepped-up power of the discovered check consists in this: one of the two vulnerable targets is the opponent's *King.*

The discovered check keeps its victim busy; meanwhile, the unmasking piece is free to venture anywhere—to capture, to threaten to capture, or to pluck off pieces by the "hit-and-run" method.

BASIC PATTERN FOR DISCOVERED CHECK

132. White moves. He will give the discovered check on the King file. In the diagram, Black's King is screened from check by the White Knight. *Any move of the Knight* will keep Black's King busy getting out of check from the unmasked White Rook.

Meanwhile the Knight will be free to capture, or threaten to capture, any important object in his range. As the most effective continuation, White chooses *1 Kt—B5ch,* attacking Black's Queen with the Knight while he opens fire on Black's King with the Rook. You will observe that *Black has no time to save his Queen!* Priority of check leaves Black no choice.

80

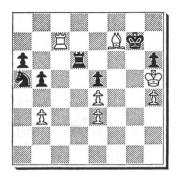

133A. White moves. His seventh rank *forms the basic pattern for a discovered check*: any move by the Bishop will discover a check by White's Rook. The problem is to find a target for the *white-squared* Bishop. This is done by *forcing the Knight to a white square*: *1 P—Kt4!*

133B. Black moves. His Knight is lost! *1 . . . Kt—Kt2?* or *1 . . . Kt—Kt6?* is out of the question. *1 . . . Kt—B5* is answered by *2 BxKtch* leaving Black no time to capture (remember the *priority of check!*). So Black tries *1 . . . Kt—B3*, but *2 B—Q5ch* wins the piece.

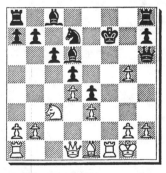

134A. White moves. He begins with a startling sacrifice: *1 Kt—B7!* forks Black's Queen and Rook. After *1 . . . KxKt* the King's Bishop file *forms the pattern for a discovered check*: *2 PxPch*. Now we see the point of the diabolical first move.

134B. Black moves. His King has been lured into *occupying the same file* as White's Rook. The King's Bishop Pawn opens the way for the Rook's gunfire and stabs at the Black Queen. However Black may play, his Queen is lost.

135A. Black moves. *Any Rook move by Black will subject his opponent to check while the Rook tries to gobble up material.* The most forceful way is *1 . . . RxPch; 2 K—Kt1, R—Kt7ch;* but after *3 K—R1,* what has White gained?!

135B. Black moves. He has altered the position slightly but *decisively.* The pattern for discovered check remains, but in a more deadly form: White's Bishop is no longer supported by a Pawn! Now comes *3 . . . R—Kt7ch; 4 K—Kt1, RxB.*

136A. Black moves. By removing the extraneous factors in complicated positions, you produce the *design for winning;* thus the "brilliant" *1 . . . QxB!* forces *2 PxQ.* What has Black achieved by the sacrifice? How will he turn it to account? By means of a discovered check.

136B. Black moves. By sacrificing his Queen, he *forced the opening of the diagonal* between Black's Bishop and White's King, creating the *basic pattern* for a discovered check. White's Queen is the biggest prey in sight, so Black pounces on it with *2 . . . R—Q1ch.*

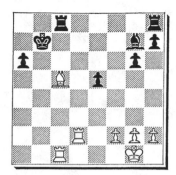

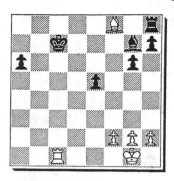

137A. White moves. He plays *1 R—Q7ch* (double attack), when *1 . . . R—B2* is compulsory. Now *2 RxRch, KxR* and we have *the basic pattern for discovered check on the Queen's Bishop file.* So: *3 B—B8ch!*

137B. Black moves. His Bishop is attacked, but cannot be saved. The Black King has been put in check by White's double-duty Bishop. Once the King moves out of check, White plays *4 BxB,* winning easily.

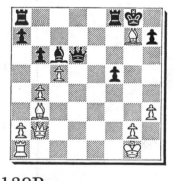

138A. White moves. His first move is a simple method of forcing a position which he has already pictured in his mind. The image derives from the *basic pattern for discovered check:*

1 **RxB!**	**QxR**
2 **BxP***ch*	**K—Kt1**
3 **P—B5***ch*	**. . . .**

138B. Black moves. His King and Queen are attacked. The King must get out of check (priority!) ; hence the Queen is lost. *White brought about this result* by creating the basic pattern for discovered check on the diagonal from his Bishop to Black's King. *White knew what he was looking for.*

QUIZ ON DISCOVERED CHECK

139. White moves. *How does he win the Queen by a discovered check?*

140. White moves. *How does he win the Queen by a discovered check?*

141. Black moves. *How does he win a piece by discovered check?*

(Solutions on page 228)

9: DOUBLE CHECK

*At the basis of every combination there shines an idea, and though combinations are without number, the number of ideas is limited—*ZNOSKO-BOROVSKY
*Let our teaching be full of ideas. Hitherto it has been stuffed only with facts—*ANATOLE FRANCE
*Even the laziest King flees wildly in the face of a double check—*NIMZOVICH

JUST AS discovered check is an intensified form of the discovered attack, so double check is an even more crushing form of discovered check. The latter is brought about by a piece which unmasks a check. In double check, the unmasking piece *also* gives check. Thus, *capture or interposition is ruled out as a defense*: the harassed King must fend for himself. Double checks are rare, but when they occur, they must be exploited to the limit. They often force checkmate directly or else score heavy gains of material.

BASIC PATTERN FOR DOUBLE CHECK

142. **Black moves.** He ignores the fact that his Queen is *en prise,* for he notes that his Queen is in line with the hostile King, separated only by a piece which can *also* give check. *This is the basic pattern for double check.* Black plays *1 . . . Kt—B6ch,* giving checkmate on the move. White cannot capture, he cannot interpose, he cannot move his King.

85

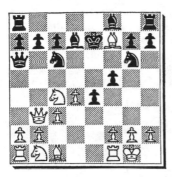

143A. **White moves.** He begins by examining possible captures and checks. *1* BxKt leads to nothing, so he turns to *1* B—Kt5*ch,* noting that Black can reply *1* . . . KxB. Can reply?!—no: *must* reply! This excites White's interest, for he sees that he *can force Black into a double check.* The play goes: *1* B—Kt5*ch!,* KxB; and now we have the pattern for a double check.

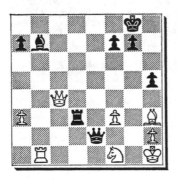

144A. **Black moves.** The mighty Bishop on the "long diagonal" leading to White's King is the star actor here. But the diagonal is momentarily blocked by a White Pawn. To suggest the obstacle is to remove it: *1* . . . RxBP! Black surrenders his Queen in order to achieve *the basic pattern for a double check.* There follows *2* QxQ, RxKt mate!

145A. **White moves.** The position of his Rook on the King's Knight file gives him an idea for constructing *the basic pattern for a double check.* The King's Knight file is now half open; do you see how it can be forced open all the way against Black's vulnerable King? The answer: *1* QxKt!, PxQ; *2* KtxKP*ch.*

143B. White moves. He completes the combination with *2 Kt—Q6 mate!* This drastic finish bears out the deadly reputation of the double check: the Knight *cannot be captured* because of the Queen check, and *interposition is impossible* because of the Knight check! All that remains is self-help: move the King. But all exits are blocked. The King is checkmated.

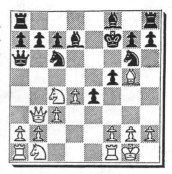

144B. Again the double check has done its deadly work. White cannot *capture* the Bishop or *interpose* to its attack, because the Rook is giving check. Similarly, the Rook's attack cannot be parried because of the Bishop check!

(Note, by the way, that after *1 . . . RxBP!* the reply *2 RxB* is answered by *2 . . . QxQ*, leaving White hopelessly behind in material.)

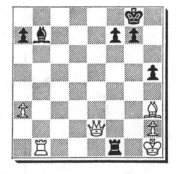

145B. Black moves. His King is doubly checked, and must move. The impudent Knight is therefore immune. After Black's King moves, there follows *3 KtxQ* and White has won a piece.

An important feature of this combination is the *unprotected* state of Black's Queen. *Loose pieces are the landmarks of combinations.*

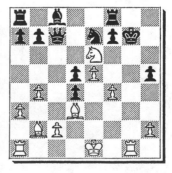

QUIZ ON DOUBLE CHECK

146. Black moves. *If he plays 1 . . . RxQ, how does White win at once?*

147. Black moves. He has just sacrificed his Queen. *How does he mate in two moves?*

(Solutions on page 229)

10: THE OVERWORKED PIECE

If the student forces himself to examine all moves that smite, however absurd they may look at first glance, he is on the way to becoming a master of tactics—PURDY
Every chess master was once a beginner—CHERNEV

THE VIEW THAT "no man can serve two masters" is often forcibly demonstrated on the chessboard. When a piece has two duties—protecting two other pieces, or protecting a piece and also guarding an important square from invasion —that piece may be *overworked*. In such situations, everything appears well defended; yet they collapse when pressure is applied to the weak point. Even tightly-knit positions, which are invulnerable to pins, Knight forks, double attacks and the like, are prone to topple on the first thrust at an overworked piece.

BASIC PATTERN FOR UNDERMINING THE OVERWORKED PIECE

148. **Black moves.** His Queen attacks a Rook, his Knight attacks the Bishop. The Knight at Q2 serves no defensive purpose, *being pinned and therefore paralyzed*. Hence White's Queen must guard the menaced pieces. To prove that the Queen is *overworked*, Black plays *1 . . . KtxBch*. After *2 QxKt* White's Queen no longer guards the Rook, so that *2 . . . QxRch* wins.

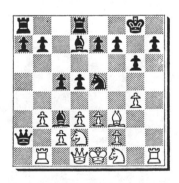

149A. White moves. Searching for a weakness in Black's position, he spots it in Black's King Pawn. This Pawn guards the Knight at Q3 (which is attacked by a White Bishop) *and also* the Bishop at KB3 (which is attacked by a White Rook). *Thus the King Pawn has a double task; it is overworked; it can be undermined.* The most logical course is *1* **BxKt** forcing *1 . . .* **PxB.**

150A. White moves. Black's pieces seem amply protected, but the fact that they are *mutually dependent on each other for support* is thought-provoking. The overworked motif may be present! Sure enough, the Rook at KR1 guards both Rook and Bishop, which are both attacked by the Rook at Kt7. The Rook at KR1 is therefore overworked. There follows *1* **RxB!**

151A. Black moves. He wants to play . . . R—K7, threatening . . . QxP mate or . . . Q—Kt7 mate. At first sight . . . R—K7 seems impossible, as the square in question is guarded by White's Rook at K1. But this Rook also has to guard the Rook at KB1, and is therefore an *overworked piece!* We undermine it with *1 . . .* **R—K7!**

149B. White moves. The overworked King Pawn has now been displaced, no longer defending the Bishop. So White continues 2 **RxB,** with a piece to the good. (Sometimes there is more than one way of undermining a piece. For example, White could have played *1* RxB, PxR; *2* BxKt with two pieces for a Rook. But *1* **BxKt** is even stronger.)

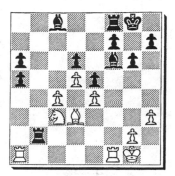

150B. Black moves. He cannot regain the lost piece! Whichever Rook is captured, his other Rook goes lost. Thus if *1* . . . R(Kt1)xR; *2* RxR or *1* . . . R(R1)xR; *2* RxR.

This combination is hard to see, for *1* **RxB!** leaves White's Rooks disunited and unprotected. *Searching for every possible capture* is particularly important against overworked pieces.

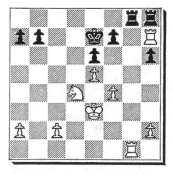

151B. White moves. He is menaced by two different mates on the second rank, and the only plausible defense 2 **RxR** allows 2 . . . **QxR** mate in reply. In Diagram 151B, White's Rook at K1 is an overworked piece; it cannot defend against every threat. The brilliant *1* . . . **R—K7!** is easy to see once we realize that the overworked piece must be undermined.

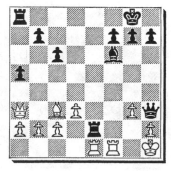

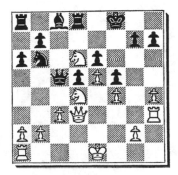

152A. White moves. There are Knight forks in the air! Following the maxim that one *must look at every check and capture,* White studies *1 KtxKtP* forking Queen and Rook. Then he notices *1 KtxPch* forking King and Queen. But in each case, the fork is guarded by Black's Bishop. *In each case?!* That is our clue! We play *1 KtxKtP!*

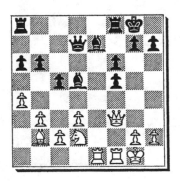

153A. White moves. His first impulse is to move away his Queen from attack. But note this: the Bishop which is doing the attacking is guarded by Black's Queen. But the other Black Bishop at K2 is also protected by the Queen from capture by White's Rook. Doesn't that make Black's Queen an *overworked piece?* And if so, shouldn't White do something about it, instead of meekly retreating? He plays *1 RxB!*

154A. Black moves. He sees that White's pinned Knight is protected by King and Queen—two pieces— and attacked by two pieces. He also sees that White's Bishop is protected by the Queen. In other words, *the protection of the Queen is common to both the Knight and Bishop.* To undermine the overworked Queen, Black plays *1 . . . BxKtch.* White replies *2 QxB.*

152B. Black moves. He sees now that his Bishop is an *overworked piece.* To get rid of the Knight fork, he plays *1 . . . BxKt (1 . . . Q—B2; 2 KtxR* is hopeless for him). Now comes *2 KtxPch,* a family check which attacks King, Queen and Rook. Black's game collapses.

The poor Bishop could not be in two places at once!

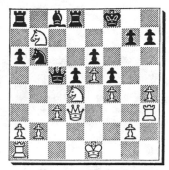

153B. Black moves. His attack on the Queen has become meaningless, as *1 . . . BxQ* is answered by *2 RxQ,* and White has gained a piece.

Therefore Black tries *1 . . . QxR* (as good as any); White continues with *2 QxBch* winning two pieces for a Rook and thus remaining with a decisive material advantage.

Again we see the value of *looking at every capture and check.*

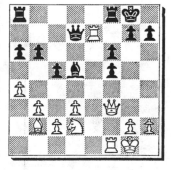

154B. Black moves. White's Queen *has been diverted from the protection of the Bishop,* so that Black can now wind up with the killing *2 . . . KtxBch,* forking King and Queen.

(Coming back to 154A, we note that Black can also win with *1 . . . Ktx Bch; 2 QxKt, BxKtch* etc.
The overworked piece can frequently be undermined in more than one way.)

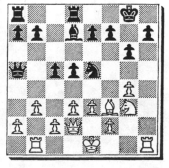

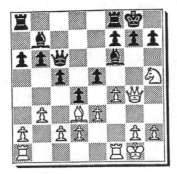

155A. White moves. Black's game looks solid, but it has weaknesses. The weak chink in his armor is the Bishop at KB3, which has to be guarded by Black's Queen; Black's King Knight Pawn, *being pinned, has no defensive value.* But Black's Queen also has to guard the Bishop at Kt2, so our problem boils down to this: how can we harry the Queen? Answer: *1 B—K4!*

156A. White moves. Once we spot the *overworked piece,* the method of *undermining* it is as delightful as it is logical. In this case it is the Black Rook at KB1 which is overworked, improbable as it may seem. This Rook has the duty of guarding the Queen and the other Rook at KR1. The undermining process begins with *1 R—Q8ch!*

157A. White moves. Is Black's Queen overworked? The Queen protects the Rook and also prevents mate at Black's KKt2. Yet the Queen is not overworked, as after *1 RxR, QxR* the mate is still guarded. *To convert the Queen into an overworked piece, it is necessary to shift the scene of the exchange of Rooks.* This is done by *1 R—R4ch.*

155B. **Black moves.** If he plays *1
. . . QxB*, then *2* KtxB*ch* forks King
and Queen. Hence Black tries *1 . . .
Q—B2* but loses a piece after *2* **BxB,
QxB;** *3* KtxB*ch* etc. (The pinned
state of the King Knight Pawn is
crucial!) *1* **B—K4!** is an ideal example
of *undermining an overworked piece*,
as the Queen can no longer guard
both Bishops. Maxim: *Disturb the
overworked piece!*

156B. **Black moves.** He is in
check, and he realizes that the checking move will draw the Rook away
from KB1, so that one of the guarded
pieces will lose its protection. Thus if
1 . . . **RxR;** *2* **QxQ** wins the Queen.
Or if *1 . . .* **K—B2;** *2* **QxQ, RxQ;** *3*
RxR with an easy win. Rarely has an
overworked piece been undermined
so artistically.

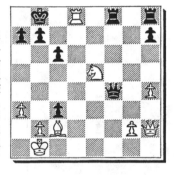

157B. **Black moves.** He finds that
the check is not easy to answer: if
1 . . . **K—Kt1;** *2* Kt—K7*ch* forks
King and Queen. He therefore interposes: *1 . . .* **R—R4.** But now the
scene of the exchange has been
shifted. The Queen must stand guard
over *two unrelated points* and thus
becomes an *overworked piece*. The
proof: *2* **RxR***ch*, **QxR;** *3* **QxP** mate.

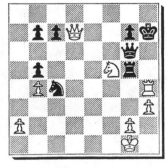

158A. White moves. Black's Rook at KR1 is chained to his post to prevent RxP mate. Consequently the Rook *may become an overworked piece.* If it is given another duty, it will crack under the strain! White plays *1 R—B8!,* relying on the fact that *1 . . . RxR?* would permit 2 Rx P mate. Black's best chance is to give up the exchange, but let us suppose he tries *1 . . . R—K1.*

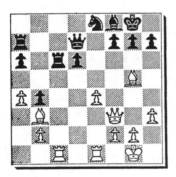

159A. White moves. He sees that the Black Queen is overworked: it has the double duty of guarding the King Bishop Pawn *and* the Rook at QB3. A capture by White *will undermine the overworked piece*—but what is the right capture? *1 RxR?,* QxR brings the Rook at R2 to the defense of the King Bishop Pawn. So we try reverse english: *1 QxPch!*

160A. White moves. The play pivots on the fact that Black's Queen is *overworked:* she defends the Knight's Pawn and also prevents Q—B8 mate. White fastens on this weakness by playing *1 RxP!* As *1 . . . Qx R?* permits 2 Q—B8 mate, Black has nothing better than *1 . . . Kt—B2.* Now his Rook at Q1 guards the mate on the last rank.

158B. White moves. He sees that Black's Rook at KR1 must now protect its brother Rook at K1 *in addition to* preventing RxP mate! Now the Black Rook is really overworked! White exploits the strained position of the Rook by 2 **RxR(K8)** and if 2 . . . **RxR;** 3 **RxP** mate.

The instructive feature here is the way that Black's Rook was *forced* to become overworked.

159B. Black moves. He must play *1 . . .* **QxQ** (if *1 . . .* K—R1??; 2 Q —Kt8 mate). Now comes 2 **BxQ***ch*, **R (or K)xB;** 3 **RxR.** White's combination has won the exchange and a Pawn.

This is a case where *transposition of moves* would spoil the whole winning process. Carelessness or lack of determination often mars such winning possibilities.

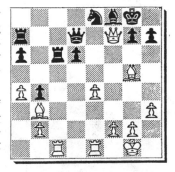

160B. White moves. True, the mate on the back rank is stopped, but White is merciless: he spots a newly created weakness in Black's camp. Black's Queen is still overworked, guarding the Knight at B2 and also parrying the threat of Q—B6*ch*, made possible by the removal of the Knight to B2. So: 2 **RxKt!,** QxR; 3 **Q—B6***ch* forcing mate!

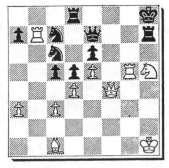

QUIZ ON THE OVERWORKED PIECE

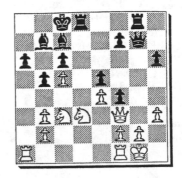

161. Black moves. White's Rook at B1 guards the other White Rook and the Bishop as well. *What capture undermines the overworked piece?*

162. Black moves. White's Queen prevents mate at KKt2 and also guards the Knight at Q3. *What capture demonstrates that the White Queen is overworked?*

163. White moves. Black's Knight at QB3 defends two pieces. *How does White prove that this Knight is overworked?*

164. White moves. Black's Queen guards two pieces. *How does White profit by this circumstance to win a piece at once?*

(Solutions on page 229)

11: REMOVING THE GUARD

We must exploit opportunities for combination whenever they are offered. Here, there is only an illusory guard, there, our opponent has a man quite unguarded, or a double attack is possible. Over and over again there occur tactical maneuvers . . . and these opportunities must frequently be created by a sacrifice—TARRASCH

NAPOLEON, who was a great general but only a mediocre chess player, coined the phrase "An army travels on its stomach" to emphasize the importance of supplying soldiers with food. Break the line of communications between soldiers and their food resources, and they are lost. On the chessboard we can think of the attacked piece as a soldier. When direct threats against it fail, *we can aim our attack against its support.* If we can destroy, drive off or exchange the guard of a piece, then *we can win that piece.*

BASIC PATTERN FOR REMOVING THE GUARD

165. **White moves.** Black's King is tied down to the defense of his Queen. If the King can be forced away, the Queen will be lost. *The most forceful move is always a check or a capture.* White plays *1 R—Kt7ch!* forcing the removal of the piece guarding the Queen. Black must play *1 . . . KxR,* whereupon *2 QxQch* is decisive.

99

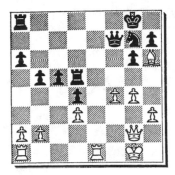

166A. **White moves.** He sees that the vulnerable point in Black's game is the Rook on Q4, guarded only by the Black Queen. With White's Queen and both Black Rooks in line, thoughts of a *double attack* suggest themselves. *The guard must be removed!* Therefore: *1* **R—K7!** This forces Black to abandon the protection of the Rook, with the continuation *1* . . . **QxR;** *2* **QxR***ch.*

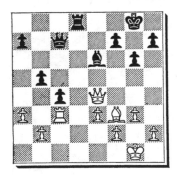

167A. **Black moves.** His point of departure is the fact that White's Bishop is guarded only by the Queen. His intention, therefore, is to harry the Queen: *1* . . . **B—Q4.** White must reply *2* **Q—Kt4** (if *2* Q—B4, Qx Q removes the guard and wins the Bishop). Now *2* . . . P—B4 looks attractive, as it apparently breaks communications between White's Queen and Bishop.

168A. **White moves.** He can play *1* **Kt—K4,** attacking the Queen with his Knight, and meanwhile discovering attack on the Knight at KB7 with his own Queen. But this would be pointless, as the Knight is guarded by the Black Bishop. "Is guarded by . . ."—there is our clue! *Remove the guard!*

1 **KtxB**   **RxKt**

166B. Black moves. The double attack costs him his Rook at QR1.

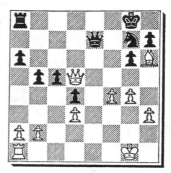

White's task in 166A was *to visualize the position with the guard (Black's Queen) removed from the board.* This led him to *1 R—K7* as the most forcible way to achieve his goal.

In chess you do not wait for things to happen—you make them happen. If not, things will happen to you.

167B. Black moves. Luckily he sees in time that *2 . . . P—B4?* is inferior, because of *3 BxBch (priority of check!)* saving the piece. Correct is *2 . . . P—KR4 removing the guard* and thus winning the Bishop.

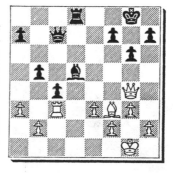

This harrying of the guard suggests to us that pieces are better protected by relatively stable Pawns than they are by pieces.

168B. White moves. Now that the Black Knight at KB7 has no protection, *2 QxKt* wins easily.

Where pieces protect pieces, the mortality rate is high! *The protecting piece is subject to exchange, capture or eviction.* As pointed out in 167B, Pawns are more sturdy defenders; uprooting them is an expensive process.

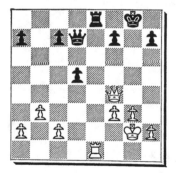

169A. White moves. He can simplify with *1 RxRch,* QxR; *2 QxP, Q —K7ch; 3 K—R3* etc., which is good enough. But he looks for a quick win, based on *removing the guard.* The indications are there, for the Black Rook, which can be captured with check, is guarded *only* by the Queen. White plays *1 Q—Kt4ch!*

170A. Black moves. His pin on the Knight would normally yield dividends by the application of more pressure—say by . . . R—K3. But he has no time, as his own Bishop is attacked. But there is a quicker course. The unhappy Knight is *protected only by pieces.* Therefore Black *removes one of the guards* with *1 . . . RxBch.*

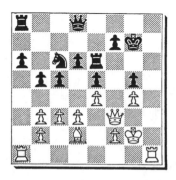

171A White moves. He has an open file for his King's Rook, and simple doubling on this file would suffice to win (*1 R—R5, R—Kt3; 2 QR—R1* etc.). But there is a quicker, more dynamic way, based on the fact that Black's defensive force is scattered: *1 R—R7ch!* The Rook *must* be captured (if *1 . . . K—Kt1?* or *1 . . . K—Kt3?; 2 QxP* mate).

169B. Black moves. To save his Queen he *must* play *1* . . . QxQ. Now White does not continue *2* Px Q? (which leaves him a Rook down after *2* . . . RxR). Instead he continues as planned: *2* RxRch, now that the Rook's defender has been removed. Black has no time to save his Queen (*priority of check!*). After *2* . . . K—Kt2; *3* PxQ wins easily.

170B. White moves. His reply is forced: *2* KxR. Now that White's Knight has lost a vital prop, Black has a *winning double attack*: *2* . . . QxKtch (*2* . . . BxKtch is also good); *3* QxQ, BxQch followed by *4* . . . B xR.

An inventory of the final position shows Black to be a piece ahead, with an easy win. The winning method here is of great practical value.

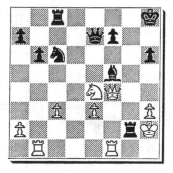

171B. Black moves. As we have shown, *1* . . . KxR is forced. But now White has removed the only defender (the Black King!) of the King Bishop Pawn, or, more exactly, of the square KB7. After *2* QxPch, Black has *2* . . . K—R1 or *2* . . . K—R3; in either event *3* R—R1ch puts Black out of his misery. In this case, *removing the guard* led to a mating attack.

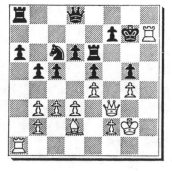

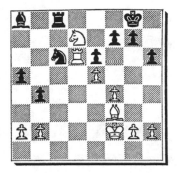

172A. White moves. He attacks the hostile Knight twice. It is defended twice. *Both guards are pieces.* If either defender can be captured or driven off, the Knight will be lost —*his guard will be removed.* These reflections lead logically to *1* **Kt— Kt6,** which forks both guards: the Rook and Bishop.

173A. Black moves. His Rook attacks White's Knight, which is defended by a Bishop. *Remove this guard* and White's position collapses. As in 172A, a Knight fork does the trick: *1 . . .* **Kt—B5.** The menaced Rook must stay on the second rank to guard the Bishop, hence *2* **R—B2.** Black is well on the way to achieving his objective.

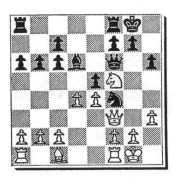

174A. White moves. He sees that the position of the hostile Knight is shaky. *It has two defenders—but both can be knocked out.* How? Not by *1* KtxB?, PxKt!; 2 PxP, PxP and the Knight is guarded by a sturdy Pawn. We need a more accurate order of moves: *1* **PxP!, QxP** (if *1* . . . BxP; *2* BxKt wins a piece). Now to *remove a guard.*

172B. **Black moves.** He plays *1
. . . R—Kt1.* This is inadequate, but
he has nothing better. Now there follows *2 KtxB, RxKt* and, amusingly
enough, neither of the Black Knight's
guards is functioning. White now captures the Knight, with a piece ahead.
Maxim: *Knock out the prop, and the
piece falls!*

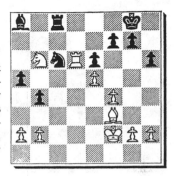

173B. **Black moves.** Has he really
come nearer to his goal? He has
blocked the action of his own Rook,
and even permitted White to increase
the Knight's protection. But, as has
been pointed out, *pieces are unstable
guards.* Now comes *2 . . . KtxB; 3 R
xKt.* Both defenders are gone; *3 . . .
RxKt* wins the piece after all. An impressive example because of its sim-
plicity.

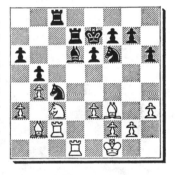

174B. **White moves.** With the
Knight guarded by two pieces, the
rest is easy: *remove one of the guards.*
The move we want is *2 KtxB,* and
whichever way Black recaptures, we
continue with *3 QxKt.*

The way in which White proves that
the Knight is *inadequately defended*
is genuinely instructive.

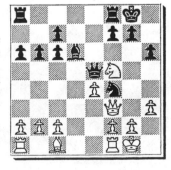

175A. White moves. His attack is concentrated against the pinned Knight. He can *remove the guard* (the King) by *1* R—R8*ch,* but after *1* . . . KxR; *2* BxKt he has lost material: the Knight is less valuable than the sacrificed Rook. But try a different order of moves: *1* **BxKt***ch!,* **QxB.**

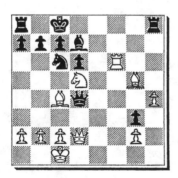

176A. White moves. Our familiarity with *removing the guard* suggests that Black's Queen, being defended by only the Knight, is in difficulties. But we must force Black's hand, else he escapes by . . . QxQ*ch.* *What we need is a forcing move which reduces Black's choice of a reply;* we look for a capture or a check. Therefore: *1* **Kt—K7***ch.*

177A. White moves. His Rook menaces Black's Bishop, which is guarded by his Knight, which in turn is guarded by a Pawn. To *remove the guard,* it is necessary to "destroy the house that Jack built" by removing the Pawn that guards the Knight that guards the Bishop.

1 **BxP***ch*   **K—B1**

175B. White moves. He has forced a position where the pinned piece (the Queen) is of greater value than the sacrificial Rook. Now 2 R—R8*ch* is successful, for it forcibly tears away Black's King from the defense of his Queen. After 2 . . . K xR; 3 QxQ White has an easy win.

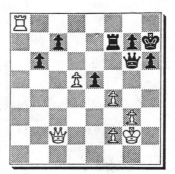

176B. Black moves. If *1* . . . Kt xKt, the Queen's guard is removed, allowing 2 QxQ. Therefore Black must play *1* . . . K—Q1 or *1* . . . K —Kt1. The problem is still *"Delenda est Carthago!"—remove the guard!* We accomplish this with another check (*priority of check!*) by playing 2 KtxKt*ch*. Now Black's defense topples. White will play *3* QxQ.

177B. White moves. He has knocked out the props from under the Knight and can now repeat the process by 2 BxKt. After 2 . . . RxB, White removes the defenseless Bishop by *3* RxB.

White's method of winning the Bishop is best described as "removing the guard of the guard."

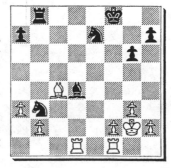

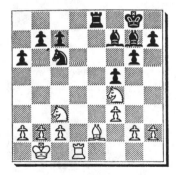

178A. Black moves. He sees that the weak link in his opponent's game is the Bishop. This piece *is guarded only by means of other pieces.* Black removes the guard by *1 . . . BxKt,* forcing *2 PxB.* White's defense is about to collapse.

178B. Black moves. He has knocked out one guard. The Pawn push *2 . . . P—KKt4* disposes of the remaining guard. White has the sad choice of moving the Knight and losing the Bishop, or of saving the Bishop and losing the Knight.

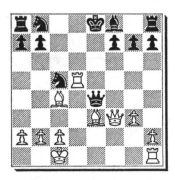

179A. White moves. He is a piece down, but can regain it with *1 QxQch, KtxQ; 2 R—K5 ch* etc. But he wants something more *forceful.* White works out a daring idea by removing the guard: *1 BxKt!!, QxQ.*

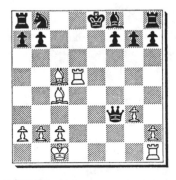

179B. White moves. He must justify his Queen sacrifice. He continues his plan: *2 R—K1 ch.* This forces *2 . . . B—K2* (interposing the Queen is useless). Now comes *3 RxBch, K—B1; 4 R—Q8* mate.

QUIZ ON REMOVING THE GUARD

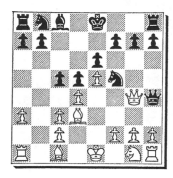

180. White moves. His Queen, now unprotected, attacks Black's Queen, which *is* protected. *Has White time to remove the guard? How?*

181. White moves. Instead of retreating his menaced Knight, he finds a way to remove the guard from the Black Rook which he attacks. *How?*

182. Black moves. *How does he win the Queen by removing its guard?*

183. Black moves. *How does he win the Queen by removing its guard?*

(Solutions on page 229)

12: "NO RETREAT"

*The idea of the combination does not have to come to us
like an inspiration from heaven. I maintain that in every
position that arises, we should deliberately search, among
other things, for any pieces which have no retreat. If we
see one, we automatically look to see if it can be netted—*
PURDY
Hang me if you like—but stop shoving me!—YOUNG
*What is immobile must suffer violence. The light-winged
bird will easily escape the huge dragon, but the firmly
rooted big tree must remain where it is and may have to
give up its leaves, fruit, perhaps even its life*—EMANUEL
LASKER

IN CHESS, we must always strive to give our pieces freedom of action. A piece that is not free to go to other squares
has no mobility—no freedom of action—and is often in
danger of being lost. An attack on it is frequently successful, for the trapped piece has lost the option of fleeing: it
has *no retreat*. In its paralyzed state, it is helpless against
the well aimed thrusts of hostile pieces.

One reason why we are constantly admonished to "cen-
tralize" pieces is that pieces occupying the center have
much more scope for action than have pieces posted at the
side of the board. This is particularly true of the Knight.

Yet centralization must not be an automatic process. A
piece in the very center of the board *whose activity is hampered by its fellow-pieces,* is exposed to the threat of attack
and capture. As for pieces at the side of the board, their
mortality rate is frightful!

BASIC PATTERN FOR "NO RETREAT"

 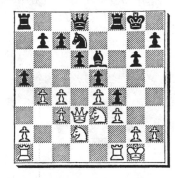

184. **Black moves.** He has an easy victim in White's Knight at the side of the board. This piece has *no retreat*. But how should the Knight's awkward situation be exploited? Should Black attack it with his Queen by *1 . . . Kt—K1?* No, for after *2 P—Kt3* the Knight would be protected.

The right way is the Pawn stab *1 . . . P—KKt4!* winning the Knight. *Against a Pawn's attack on a piece, neither exchange nor protection can be satisfactory.*

185. **White moves.** His Knight at K3 is attacked. He can move it safely to Q1 or QB2. But suppose he becomes thoughtlessly aggressive, and wants to post the Knight at Q5? The Knight would then have no flight-square—*no retreat.* Black would play *1 . . . P—B3* winning the Knight.

These two examples illustrate the power of the "weak" Pawn in this type of attack. *Flight, when possible, is generally the only defense to a Pawn's attack.*

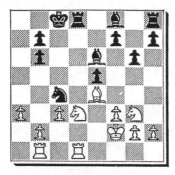

186. **Black moves.** He is immediately struck by the fact that White's Bishop has *no retreat*. It cannot go forward, while flight is blocked by its own pieces. A *Pawn* attack will be painful: *1 . . . P—B4* wins the Bishop at once. Such situations often turn up in practical play.

187. **Black moves.** What feature, above all, stands out in this position? *White's Queen does not have a single move!* The Queen, having *no retreat*, is an easy prey to attack. Black hits out at the paralyzed Queen with the immediately decisive *1 . . . Kt—R5!* White resigns!

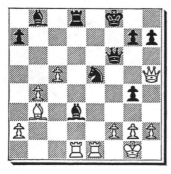

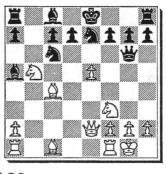

188. **Black moves.** The hostile Queen has *no retreat*. To win the Queen, *it is sufficient to attack it with any piece of lesser value.* This hint yields us *1 . . . B—Kt3*, winning the Queen. After *2 RxRch, QxR* White has no relief.

189. **White moves.** The candidate for destruction is Black's Queen, which has an off-side position with few flight squares, while White's minor pieces have great freedom of action. *1 Kt—R4* does the trick, leaving the Queen *14* untouchable squares!

190. **White moves.** A Knight has least mobility at the side of the board. Black's Knight has only one flight square: KKt8. The logical course is therefore *1 K—B1.* White follows this up with *2 K—Kt2,* winning the Knight, which has *no retreat.*

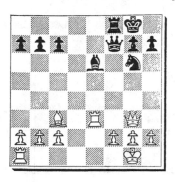

191. **Black moves.** This position is an example of one of the most common *no retreat* patterns: Black's Bishop goes Pawn-snatching and soon finds itself in a *cul-de-sac.* He plays *1 . . . Bx P?* But with *2 P—Kt3* the steel trap closes on the Bishop, which has *no retreat.*

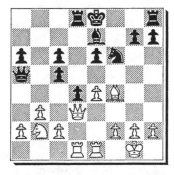

192. **Black moves.** He plays *1 . . . QxP?* under the impression that his attack on the Knight will give him the needed time to retreat the Queen to safety. But *2 Kt—B4* closes the exit gate. Black's Queen has no retreat and will be won by *3 R—R1.*

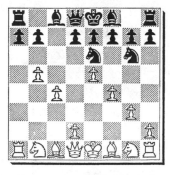

193. **Black moves.** His Knights are menaced by the threat of P—KB5. If *1 . . . Kt—B4; 2 P—B5!, KtxP; 3 P—Q4* forking the Knights. Or *1 . . . Kt—B2; 2 P—KB5!, KtxP; 3 P—Q4* and there is no retreat for the Knight of the Rueful Countenance.

194A. Black moves. His King Bishop Pawn requires protection. Instead of resorting to passive defense, he prefers to counterattack. This takes the form of exploiting the awkward position of White's Bishop and his Knight on KKt4. When fleeing from attack, they are bound to get in each other's way:

1	P—KKt4!
2 B—Kt3	P—KR4!

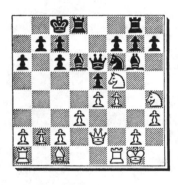

195A. White moves. Tarrasch has said: "No piece can be so easily won by Pawns as a Bishop." The target here is Black's Bishop at KKt3. White intends to surround it with Pawns. He begins with *1* KtxB*ch*, **Qx Kt** (if *1* . . . PxKt; *2* P—B5 with double attack). The sequel is easy.

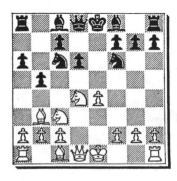

196A. Black moves. This position from the Ruy Lopez is so old that it is known as the "Noah's Ark" Trap. As in 195A, the hemming-in process is used to trap a Bishop. *Knowing what to look for*, Black begins with a *forcible move*, a capture: *1* . . . **Ktx Kt;** *2* **QxKt.** Now another forcible move, a threat: *2* . . . **P—B4** attacking White's Queen.

194B. White moves. The menaced Knight must retreat, and he has only one square for the purpose: KR2. But by going there (*3 Kt—R2*), he robs the Bishop of its only flight square. Now *3 . . . P—R5* strikes at the helpless Bishop, which has *no retreat* and is therefore lost. This is an elaboration of the much simpler position in Diagram 186, where the Bishop obviously had no retreat. Here his flight is prevented.

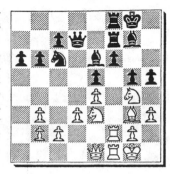

195B. White moves. He executes his plan with *2 P—B5* forcing *2 . . . B—R4*. Now *3 P—KKt4* wins the Bishop, which is attacked and has *no retreat*. Trapping a Bishop inside a web of Pawns is a fairly frequently seen stratagem. It has some similarity to the method used in Diagram 191.

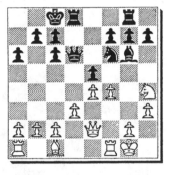

196B. White moves. Now he sees the coming threat to his Bishop, but he has no choice: he must save his Queen. Once the Queen retreats, *3 . . . P—B5* closes in on the Bishop, leaving it *no retreat*.

Aside from its practical value, this trap teaches the importance of preparatory *forcing* moves.

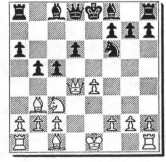

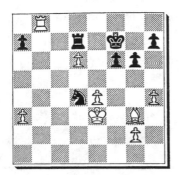

197A. Black moves. He goes after a stray Pawn at the side of the board: *1 . . . Kt—B7ch?* After *2 K—Q3* (moving in for the kill), Black is forced to do what he wants to do: *2 . . . KtxP.*

197B. White moves. He is well satisfied with the position: the Black Knight has no moves —*no retreat!* White swoops down with *3 R—Kt3*, attacking and winning the miserable Knight.

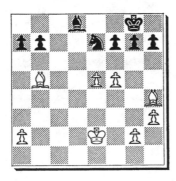

198A. Black moves. He goes in for a tempting but unsound combination. Relying on a "clever" Knight fork, he wins a Pawn: *1 . . . KtxP?; 2 BxB, Kt—Q5ch; 3 K—Q3, KtxB.* Thus Black has regained the sacrificed piece and is a Pawn to the good. It is a case of " 'Will you come into my parlor?' said the spider."

198B. White moves. His opponent has won a Pawn, but the Knight is stranded on a square where it has little mobility. Again we have the drama of *no retreat*:

4 **P—QR4**	**Kt—R6**
5 **B—K7**	**Kt—Kt8**
6 **K—B2**	. . . .

The Knight is lost!

QUIZ ON "NO RETREAT"

199. White moves. One of Black's pieces has no mobility. Which Pawn move by White will win this piece?

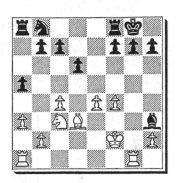

200. White moves. *What moves must you make to (a) cut off the retreat of Black's Bishop and (b) win the Bishop?*

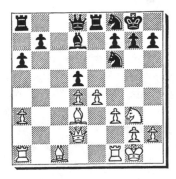

201. White moves. Black's pieces stand in each other's way. *How does White win a piece?*

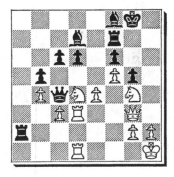

202. White moves. Black's Queen has no mobility—*no retreat. What move wins the Queen?*

(Solutions on pages 229–230)

13: THE SKEWER

The Middle Game is chess in excelsis, the most beautiful part of the game, in which a lively imagination can exercise itself most fully and creatively in conjuring up magnificent combinations—TARRASCH
The pleasure of a chess combination lies in the feeling that a human mind is behind the game, dominating the inanimate pieces with which the game is carried on, and giving them the breath of life—RETI

THE SKEWER is a piercing attack which menaces two hostile pieces placed on the same line. As the piece directly attacked moves away, the piece behind it is transfixed on the skewer.

B. H. Wood, who credits the invention of this term to Edgar Pennell, contrasts the skewer with another common kitchen utensil: "Just as a fork is something with more than one prong which can stick into two lumps of meat on your plate at the same time, so the skewer is something that pushes right through a lump of meat, and out the other side."

A penetrating, "follow-through" attack, the skewer has an effectiveness which is queerly pleasurable. We get a taste of it as children when we set up a row of toy soldiers a little distance apart from each other, and then give the one in front a push. He falls backwards, giving the same motion to the one behind him. He does the same to the soldier behind him, until they have all fallen down. How odd it seems that a slight touch can "follow through" to knock over the last soldier in the line! So it is with the skewer.

To sum up: the skewer attack operates by piercing through a piece in order to transfix another *on the same straight line*. It is the second piece which is therefore the real target. Opportunities to bring about the skewer may present themselves whenever two enemy pieces are in line on the same file, rank or diagonal.

BASIC PATTERN FOR THE SKEWER

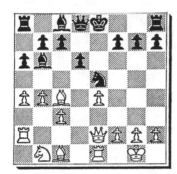 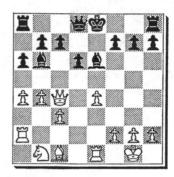

203A. Black moves. He sees an opportunity for a skewer attack in the diagonal placement of White's Bishop on QB4 and his Rook at QR2. The two pieces are *in line,* and there ought to be a way . . .

1 . . . B—K3 is pointless, as *2* BxB can be played. What we need is the substitution of White's Queen for the Bishop at QB4. It is very easily arranged: *1 . . .* KtxB; *2* QxKt, B—K3. This is the desired position.

203B. White moves. He is trapped in a classic example of the skewer attack. The previous exchange placed two of White's *major pieces in line* on the same diagonal. *Major pieces always make good targets,* as they can rarely afford capture when menaced by minor pieces. White must discreetly withdraw the Queen; after *3* Q—K2, BxR; *4* QxB etc. he has lost the exchange without any compensation.

204A. Black moves. He can create a skewer attack by forcing the *substitution* of White's King for White's Bishop. In that case, White will be susceptible to a powerful check by Black's Bishop. Now for the mechanics: we start with a *forcing* move, therefore *1* . . . **RxBch**. White must recapture: *2* **KxR**.

205A. White moves. He pins the Black Bishop, and he can strengthen the pin with *1* B—B3 or *1* B—B2. But then comes *1* . . . R—Kt8*ch;* *2* B—K1, P—B7 and *Black's* pin wins!

Considering every possible capture or check, White hits on the right idea: a skewer attack!

   1 **RxB***ch!*   **KxR**

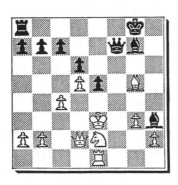

206A. Black moves. His opponent's King and Queen *are in line* on the diagonal. Is a skewer attack possible? Apparently not, as White's Bishop guards the critical diagonal. But if we can drive the Bishop off, then the skewer will be possible. Therefore: *1* . . . **Q—B4.** The White Bishop cannot be protected, so White plays *2* **B—R4.**

204B. Black moves. He has brought about a position where two major enemy pieces occupy the same diagonal—an ideal target for the skewer. Black plays 2 . . . **B—Kt5ch**. After White moves his King away, 3 . . . **BxR** leaves Black a piece ahead. The Rook was the real target of Black's combination.

205B. White plays. By sheer force, he has produced a position ripe for the skewer. Black's King and Rook *are in line* on the diagonal. White strikes at both pieces with 2 **B—B2ch**. After Black's King moves, White captures the Rook with a piece ahead. Again the Rook was the target.

206B. Black moves. The hindrance to the skewer has been driven off, so that 2 . . . **B—R3ch** is now possible. This attacks not only the King, but White's Queen as well. White must play 3 **Kt—B4**, allowing 3 . . . **PxKt*ch*** with complete collapse. (White's Queen will now be lost just the same. How?)

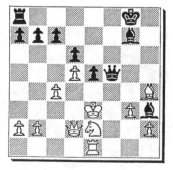

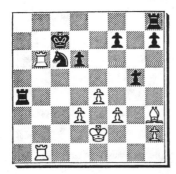

207A. White moves. If he can *force* Black's King back to the first rank, the Rook at KR1 will become the *real target* for a skewer attack. Forcing moves are usually checks or captures: White begins with *1* **R—Kt7***ch,* **K—Q1.**

Now Black has King and Rook in line, making a skewer attack feasible. But there is a difficulty!

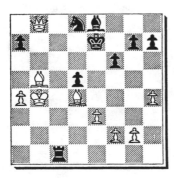

208A. Black moves. He is so far behind in material (Rook for Queen) that only a miracle can save him. The miracle is available, for the White King and Queen are in line, making possible a skewer in veiled form. At the moment *1* . . . R—Kt8*ch* is meaningless, as White's Bishop on Kt5 stops the skewer. The Bishop must be removed: *1* . . . **Kt—B3***ch!*

209A. White moves. He has two possible captures: *1* KxB (which wins) or *1* QxR (which loses). Like Portia's suitors, he makes the wrong choice: *1* **QxR.** The move looks attractive, for it threatens mate and leaves Black with (apparently) nothing but a desperate check or two. But Black heads straight for a skewer!—*1* . . . **Q—R8** *ch; 2* **K—Kt3, QxP***ch; 3* **K—B4.**

207B. White moves. He would like to play 2 R—Kt8*ch* (the skewer!) but is prevented by Black's Knight. He studies the position some more. His Rooks are doubled on the file, so why fear the Knight capture? White continues the planned attack: 2 R—Kt8*ch!*, KtxR; 3 RxKt*ch*, K—K2; 4 RxR. The skewer has impaled Black's Rook after all!

208B. White moves. As his King and Queen are menaced by the Knight fork, he must reply 2 BxKt. But with the Bishop off the Queen's Knight file, the *skewer* is now feasible: 2 . . . R—Kt8*ch*. White must get his King out of check, losing the Queen and the game.

The combination of fork and skewer is quite artistic.

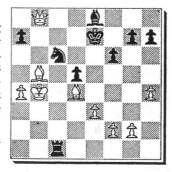

209B. Black moves. He has driven White's King to the King's Bishop file, so that both their majesties are in line. With the chief actors in their proper places, we are ready for the skewer: 3 . . . Q—B6*ch*. White's King must step aside, letting the skewer penetrate to his Queen (4 . . . QxQ).

This example and 208B show the value of the skewer for counterattack.

210A. Black moves. He threatens mate at KKt7, but this is prevented by White's Queen. But at QB2 the Queen is undefended, which gives Black the idea of trying to work out a skewer attack. He needs *forcing* moves for this, and he has them: plenty of checks.

1	QxP*ch*
2 K—Kt1	Q—R8*ch*
3 K—B2	. . . .

211A. Black moves. As we know, the favorable elements for a skewer attack are in evidence. White's Queen is unguarded; his King can be *forced* back to the second rank, where it will be in line with the White Queen. Play proceeds logically:

1	Q—R8*ch*
2 K—Kt3	P—R5*ch!*
3 K—B2	. . . .

212A. White moves. We look for *forcing* moves, noting that Black has only a limited number of King moves in reply. In such situations the defender is generally helpless to change the inexorable course of events, and he is frequently forced into a skewer position. We begin with *1* Q—Q7*ch,* K—R3 (other King moves allow a mate in one); *2* Q—Kt7*ch,* K—R4.

210B. **Black moves.** He has brought about the desired position by means of two *checks*. Now comes the skewer with 3 . . . **Q—R7***ch* (or, if you wish, 3 . . . **Q—Kt7***ch*—a matter of taste). After White's King moves, Black plays 4 . . . **QxQ** and it is all over. This type of skewer attack is quite frequent and deserves careful study. See 211A for a very similar procedure.

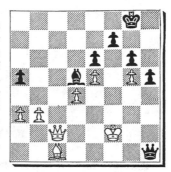

211B. **Black moves.** What now follows is clearly indicated. He has driven White's King and Queen *into the same line*. An attack on the King will penetrate and find its mark in the unprotected Queen. Black plays 3 . . . **Q—R7***ch;* White's King moves off the rank; Black captures the Queen, winning at once.

In 212A the same idea appears in a more elaborate form.

212B. **White moves.** He is almost ready now for the skewer, aimed at Black's Queen. First 3 **Q—R7***ch,* forcing 3 . . . **K—Kt5.** Now Black's King and Queen are in line—the maximum objective of a skewer attack. White plays 4 **QxP***ch,* and the attack pierces through to win the unfortunate Black Queen, as White ends up with 5 **QxQ.**

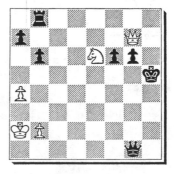

QUIZ ON THE SKEWER

213. White moves. Black's Queen and Bishop are in line on the Queen's Bishop file. *How does White win a piece by the skewer?*

214. White moves. Black's King and Queen are in line on a rank. *How does White win the Queen by the skewer attack?*

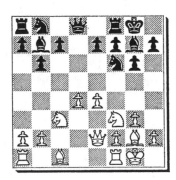

215. Black moves. White's Queen and Rook (at KB1) are on the same diagonal. *How does Black win the exchange by the skewer attack?*

216. Black moves. *How does he force Black's King and Queen into the same line, in order to win by the skewer attack?*

(Solutions on page 230)

14: QUEENING COMBINA-TIONS

Every Pawn is a potential Queen—MASON
The Passed Pawn is a criminal, who should be kept under lock and key. Mild measures, such as police surveillance, are not sufficient—NIMZOVICH
A Passed Pawn increases in strength as the number of pieces on the board diminishes—CAPABLANCA
Any material change in a position must come about by mate, a capture, or a Pawn-promotion—PURDY

THE COMPLICATIONS of the middle-game frequently result in the exchange of a great many pieces. The players then reach the end-game stage with too few *pieces* to try for checkmate. It stands to reason that one side with Rook, Knight and four Pawns can hardly force checkmate against an opponent who has Rook, Knight and three Pawns.

How, then, do you win an end-game? *There is generally only one way to win an ending.* That way is to create an advantage in material so great that further resistance on your adversary's part becomes absurd.

How can you achieve this objective? *By advancing a Pawn to the eighth rank, where it can be promoted to a Queen.* This piece is the mating force *par excellence*, so that if you are a Queen ahead, the method of forcing a win presents no problem. The Queen either (*a*) carries through a direct mating attack; or (*b*) captures all your opponent's remaining pieces and Pawns.

How can one of your Pawns become a fit candidate for promotion to a Queen? *It must be converted into a Passed Pawn*—it must have no enemy Pawns disputing its forward march on the same file, or on either of the adjacent

127

files; and it must not be blocked by one of its own **Pawns**.

How do you exploit the advantage of a Passed Pawn? *To make the Passed Pawn a fit candidate for queening, you must push the Passed Pawn at every available opportunity.* Every step forward by the Passed Pawn brings it that much nearer to its goal (the eighth rank), and creates more and more critical problems for the enemy. As the Pawn approaches the queening-square, your opponent's attention is necessarily diverted to the problem of *blockading* your Passed Pawn.

The technique of playing endings (this includes 99% of all endings) can be boiled down to these simple rules:

1 Get a Passed Pawn!

2 Push the Passed Pawn!

3 Clear the way for the Passed Pawn to advance.

4 Capture, exchange or drive off any blockader of the Passed Pawn.

5 When the Passed Pawn has a clear road to the queening-square, *simplify* by exchanging all the pieces on the board, sacrificing material if necessary.

Observing these rules does not mean that you are to abandon all other tactics and strategy. It does mean that you must push the Passed Pawn every time there is an opportunity to do so.

You must avoid advancing the Passed Pawn recklessly. Your opponent will attempt to interrupt its progress by placing a piece (blockader) in its path. Or he will threaten the Passed Pawn with capture in the event that it marches forward.

Your problem will then be how to get rid of the blockader; or how to control the squares leading to the queening-square; or possibly how to exchange the remaining pieces of both sides, so that the lone survivor, the Passed Pawn, can march in triumph to its coronation.

BASIC PATTERN FOR QUEENING COMBINATIONS

217A. White moves. Following the basic rule for the handling of Passed Pawns, he plays *1 P—B7. Passed Pawns must be pushed!* White threatens to advance the Pawn now to the queening-square. The only way Black can prevent this is to give up his Queen for the Pawn. Whichever course he takes, White remains a whole Rook ahead, with (of course) an easy win.

How did all this come about? Was it luck, or an application of end-game principles? Diagram

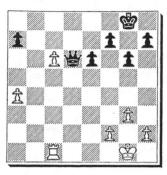

217B shows the position a few moves earlier. Let us see how White (the great master Capablanca) evolved his winning plan.

217B. White moves. His Passed Pawn does not look very formidable. The Black Queen and Rook half-surround it. But that in itself is an important point! *One "mere" Pawn keeps two such powerful pieces as Black's Queen and Rook occupied in preventing its further advance.*

How does White remove the blockading Black Queen? Not by waiting for the Queen to go away, nor by wishful thinking. The Queen must be *forced* to move. Once more we search for a *violent* move: *a capture or a check.* White plays *1 Q—K5ch.* Black replies *1 . . . K—Kt1*

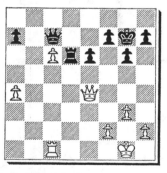

(other moves do not affect the outcome). Now White plays another *violent* move, this time a capture: *2 QxR!* Black recaptures: *2 . . . QxQ,* giving the position of 217A. The Pawn is free, the road is clear, the win easy.

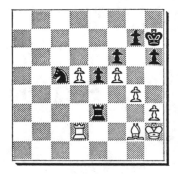

218A. **White moves.** He has a Passed Pawn on the Queen file. His course is clear: advance the Pawn! Hence *1* **P—Q6,** threatening *2* P—Q7. Black dare not defend with *1 . . .* R —Q6, for then *2* RxR, KtxR; *3* P— Q7 and the Passed Pawn becomes a Queen. Therefore Black *blockades the Passed Pawn* with *1 . . .* **Kt— Q2.** White promptly *attacks the blockader* with *2* **B—B6.**

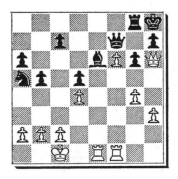

219A. **White moves.** He has a Passed Pawn on KB6, but apparently there is no way to advance it. Black's Queen blockades its advance; the Black Bishop exerts pressure on the next square of the Pawn's march; Black's Rook guards the last rank. But White applies the magic formula: *Remove the blockader!*

    1 **RxB!**   **QxR**

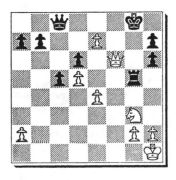

220A. **White moves.** He has many winning lines, but the great Paul Morphy, famous for the elegance of his attacking play, naturally seeks the quickest way. His King's Pawn is already advanced to the seventh rank. What stops its promotion? The Black Queen. *Therefore that piece must be removed,* and here is how it is done: *1* Q—K6*ch!*, **QxQ** (forced); *2* **PxQ.**

218B. **Black moves.** Alas, his blockader (the Knight at Q2) must leave his post: *2 . . . Kt—Kt1,* attacking the Bishop. White replies *3 B—K8, controlling the next square in the Pawn's path.* Thus all further blockade is impossible. After *4 P—Q7,* Black will have to give up his Knight for the Pawn to prevent it from queening. The extra piece will win easily.

219B. **White moves.** The two obstacles to the Passed Pawn's advance have been thrust aside, and the Pawn (which should have been kept "under lock and key") advances: *2 P—B7! Passed Pawns must be pushed!* Black is helpless against the specter of the Pawn's promotion. There followed: *2 . . . R—Q1; 3 P—B8(Q)ch, RxQ; 4 RxRch* winning the Queen.

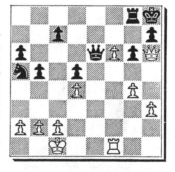

220B. **Black moves.** He finds himself in an exquisitely painful situation. The Passed Pawn threatens to become a Queen, and Black is powerless to do *anything* about it! His Rook can do nothing, his King cannot go to KB2.

White knew that the *Pawn had to be pushed;* he knew that the obstacle had to be removed. This amusing tableau is the consequence.

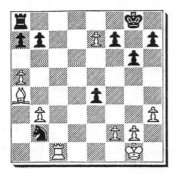

221A. Black moves. He is confronted with the imminent queening of White's Passed Pawn. *As the queening-square is covered by White's Bishop,* the promotion of the Passed Pawn will cost Black his Rook. He therefore plays *1 . . . KtxB,* intending to answer the obvious *2 PxKt* with . . . R—K1—after which the worst will have been avoided.

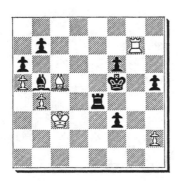

222A. Black moves. He wants to push his Passed Pawn to KB7 and KB8, acquiring a Queen. But White's Bishop at QB5 prevents the advance of the Passed Pawn. *1 . . . R—KB5* looks like a good try, but then *2 B—B2* stops the Passed Pawn. We must proceed according to the slogan *Remove the blockader!* The right way is *1 . . . R—B5ch.* White plays *2 K—Q2* edging nearer to the dangerous Passed Pawn.

223A. Black moves. There is no Passed Pawn yet. But by means of a startling sacrifice Black will create a Passed Pawn. Then, according to principle, *he will advance the Passed Pawn to the queening-square.* He begins with *1 . . . Kt—B5ch,* forcing *2 K—B2.* Now he creates the Passed Pawn with *2 . . . KtxP!*

221B. White moves. But he does not care to play the obvious recapture! He studies the situation: he has a Passed Pawn, and *Passed Pawns must be pushed!* What stops the Pawn from queening? The Rook. Therefore the Rook *must be removed!* White plays 2 **R—Q1**! (threat: 3 R—Q8*ch,* RxR; 4 PxR[Q]*ch* and wins). Black tries 2 . . . **R—K1** but must lose after 3 **R—Q8**! pinning.

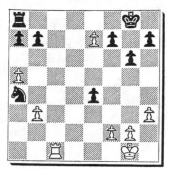

222B. Black moves. And now, according to plan, he *destroys the blockader*: 2 . . . **RxB**. After 3 PxR comes the point of the sacrifice of the exchange: 3 . . . **P—B7**. Note that 4 K—K2 and 4 R—Kt1 are both impossible. Hence White has no way to stop the Passed Pawn from advancing to the last rank and becoming a Queen.

In 223A the blockader is removed even more drastically.

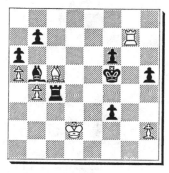

223B. White moves. Having no better reply, he accepts the sacrifice by 3 **KtxKt**. In return for the piece, Black has a powerful Passed Pawn. He advances it at once: 3 . . . **P—R6**. No matter how White plays now, *he cannot prevent the Passed Pawn from queening!* (Prove this.) Another clever Capablanca ending.

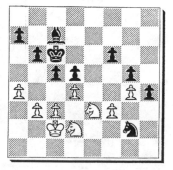

224A. **Black moves.** The imminent promotion of his Passed Pawn on the Queen's Knight file is prevented by White's Queen, which acts as "goal-keeper." To break through the defense, *it is necessary for Black to control the queening-square.* Hence he plays *1 . . . Q—K5ch,* so that if 2 K—Kt1, P—Kt8(Q), he is a whole Queen ahead! White tries 2 **P—B3.**

225A. **Black moves.** He would like to queen his Passed Pawn without loss of time. But see all the difficulties: *White's Knight controls the queening-square;* his King threatens to advance toward the precious Pawn and capture it; finally, Black's Bishop is attacked. But one startling move changes the picture: *1 . . . B—Kt7!*

226A. **Black moves.** He has a considerable advantage in material, and his Passed Pawn has a clear road ahead of it. But advancing the Passed Pawn is premature, for example *1 . . . P—Q7?;* 2 R—Kt7ch, K—R1 (not *2 . . . K—R3??;* 3 Kt—Kt8 mate!); *3* R—Kt8ch and Black's King cannot escape the perpetual check. Relying on the Passed Pawn, he plays *1 . . . Q—Kt5ch!*

224B. **Black moves.** His Queen is attacked. Instead of moving it away, he observes the maxim *Passed Pawns must be pushed!* He therefore plays *2 ... P—Kt8(Q)*, for now White's Queen is also attacked. If *3 PxQ, QxQch.* No matter what White does on his third move, he must remain a Queen behind. Note the immediately decisive effect of *controlling the queening-square.*

225B. **White moves.** His hopes have been dashed. His Knight is an *overworked piece*: if *2 KtxB, P—B8 (Q)ch.* The Bishop is tabu, but he *controls the queening-square;* so that if *2 K—K2* (trying to approach the Passed Pawn), *P—B8(Q); 3 KtxQ, Bx Kt* and Black's material advantage gives him an easy win. A Passed Pawn is no longer a "humble" or "lowly" Pawn.

226B. **White moves.** He has no good continuation. If *2 K—R2, Qx R; 3 KtxQ, KxKt* and White cannot prevent the Passed Pawn from marching on to become a Queen. No better for White is *2 RxQ, PxRch.* If White were not in check now, he could play *3 Kt—Q5* or *3 Kt—B5*, followed by *4 Kt—K3* stopping the Passed Pawn. But *priority of check* forces White to play a King move, allowing *3 ... P —Q7* etc.

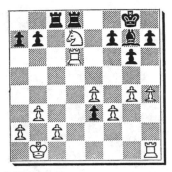

227A. Black moves. He has a deep plan for making use of his Passed Pawn on K6. He begins with *1 . . . R—B2,* intensifying the pin on the Knight. *2 Kt—B6ch* is refuted by *2 . . . BxKt; 3 RxB, P—K7* (threatens *4 . . . R—Q8ch,* as in 221B); *4 K—B1, R(B2)—Q2* and wins. White therefore tries *2 R(R1)— Q1.* Momentarily his Knight is adequately guarded.

227B. Black moves. He has two ways of utilizing his Passed Pawn. One is: *2 . . . P—K7,* making White's attacked Rook *an overworked piece.* If it moves on the file, then the Pawn advances and becomes a Queen; if the Rook moves on the rank, then White's Knight is lost. The second method is: *2 . . . R(B2)x Kt; 3 RxR, RxR; 4 RxR, P—K7!* and queens.

228A. White moves. In 226 and 227 we have seen the value of simplifying in order to exploit the strength of a Passed Pawn. Here the combination begins with *1 QxR!* forcing *1 . . . PxQ.*

228B. White moves. Now comes more simplification: *2 Rx Bch, QxR; 3 BxQ.* If here *3 . . . KtxRP; 4 BxKt* and White is a whole Rook ahead. However, on *3 . . . KxB; 4 P—R7* is decisive.

QUIZ ON QUEENING COMBINATIONS

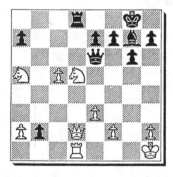

229. **White moves.** His Passed Pawn is prevented from advancing by Black's King. *How does he drive off the blockader and win the game?*

230. **Black moves.** His Passed Pawn is prevented from advancing to the queening-square by White's Bishop. *How does Black get rid of the Bishop?*

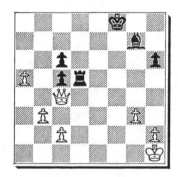

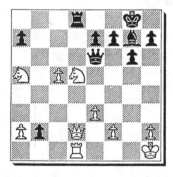

231. **White moves.** He is ahead in material and has several ways of winning. The quickest method is *to simplify by sacrificing,* so that his Passed Pawn can march on irresistibly. *How does White accomplish this?*

232. **Black moves.** This position will be recognized as a "relative" of 224. *How can Black clear away most of the pieces in order to reach a simplified position in which his Passed Pawn can advance victoriously?*

(Solutions on page 230)

15: THE VULNERABLE FIRST RANK

If a Rook is tied to the back rank to prevent mate, anything seemingly protected by it on the file can be taken
—PURDY

The knowledge which we have acquired ought not to resemble a great shop without order, and without an inventory; we ought to know what we possess, and be able to make it serve us in need—LEIBNITZ

"CASTLE EARLY and often!" is the way one wit put it, to emphasize the necessity of getting the King into safety as quickly as possible.

Of the two methods of castling, the King-side is preferable in the great majority of cases; but even there, the King is not quite secure. He is hemmed in by his own Pawns, and cannot advance; yet, being posted on the first rank, he cannot retreat! *It is therefore logical to conclude that the King is vulnerable to checks by Rook or Queen on the critical first rank.*

This leads to a very natural question: why not assure the King's safety by advancing one of the Pawns in front of him, in order to create an escape (a "loophole") for His Majesty? In the end-game stage, such an advance of one of the Pawns is usually in order. During the middle-game, however, it is inadvisable to disturb the position of the Pawns in front of the castled King. An alteration in the Pawn position creates weaknesses which allow hostile pieces to occupy threatening posts whence they can no longer be driven away by Pawns.

BASIC PATTERN FOR THE VULNERABLE FIRST RANK

233A. *Black is checkmated.* Offhand it might seem that he had been a bit careless and overlooked the mate pictured in the diagram. That this is not the case, can be seen from the next diagram, which shows how this position came about. Later on, we shall see that the weakness of the first rank often makes remarkable combinations possible. Sometimes the result is outright mate, as here; other times, exploitation is indirect.

233B. White moves. Spotting the weakness of Black's first rank, he plays *1 QxR!* The sacrifice is decisive, because it removes one of the defenders of Black's first rank. After *1 . . . RxQ* Black has only one Rook guarding his Q1, while White has two Rooks trained on it. There follows: *2 R—Q8ch, RxR; 3 RxR* mate, as in 233A. In such situations, the creation of a "loophole" by (say) . . . P—KR3 is advisable.

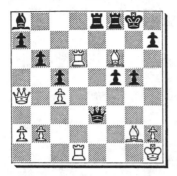

234A. Black moves. His Queen and a Rook are trained on White's first rank, which is guarded by a Rook and Bishop. But the Bishop, *being pinned, is paralyzed.* Therefore the first rank is *vulnerable to attack.* Black can invade by sacrificing his Queen: *1 . . . Q—K8ch!* forcing *2 RxQ.*

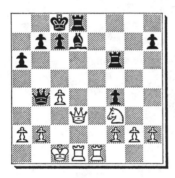

235A. White moves. It seems difficult if not impossible to penetrate Black's first rank. Yet it can be done; and *if we look for all possible checks and captures,* we find the violent move *1 QxBch!* Black plays *1 . . . RxQ* (*1 . . . K—Kt1* avoids mate but leads to frightful loss of material).

236A. White moves. He attacks the King Rook Pawn twice, and it is defended only once. Not realizing *that his Queen is tied to the defense of the first rank,* he plays *1 RxRP?* With this capture, White's first rank becomes vulnerable. To prove this, Black sacrifices his Queen with *1 . . . QxR!* As he cannot remain a Rook down, White retakes: *2 QxQ.*

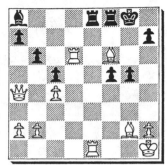

234B. **Black moves.** He recaptures with his Rook, and White is checkmated! Of course White's Bishop must not interpose.

Since a *vulnerable first rank implies mating possibilities,* it often permits the most fantastic sacrifices of material. See 244A!

235B. **White moves.** He continues with *occupation of the vulnerable rank*: 2 R—K8*ch.* Black must interpose by 2 . . . R—Q1. Now either White Rook captures the Rook, giving checkmate. The brilliant sacrifice *1 QxBch!* was perpetrated in actual play by Paul Keres on World Champion Alekhine.

236B. **Black moves.** He swoops down the whole length of the open file: 2 . . . R—B8*ch.* White interposes with *3* R—B1; perhaps he overlooks the long-range effect of Black's Bishop at QR3! Black now follows through with 3 . . . RxR mate. (Had White played *3* Q—Q1, he would have delayed the mate for one move.) The Queen sacrifice was startling but logical.

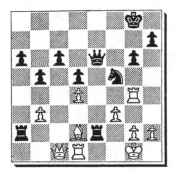

237A. **Black moves.** He wants to invade White's first rank via the King file. The play in 235A tells us what to look for. *Searching for forcing moves such as checks or captures,* Black decides in favor of *1 . . . R (R7)xB.* White recaptures by *2 RxR.* (If *2 QxR, RxQ; 3 RxR, Q—K8* mate!)

238A. **White moves.** His Queen and Rook are doubled on the Queen Bishop file—one of the surest methods of dominating an open line. Such control enables one to use the file as a "jumping-off place" for forcible entry into the hostile position. The opponent's first rank is a favorite target for this type of attack. White plays *1 B—Kt3* with a double threat.

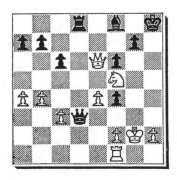

239A. **Black moves.** It is not clear how he can work up an attack against White's first rank. But the process of looking for checks and captures again gives us a priceless hint. We begin with *1 . . . P—B6ch,* which forces White's King to Kt1 in order to keep the Rook guarded. *Now White's first rank is vulnerable.* The search for checks and captures yields a delightful sequel: *2 . . . QxRch!*

237B. Black moves. By sacrificing the exchange, he has rendered White's *first rank vulnerable to invasion.* Two of the defenders of White's K1 are gone, so that Black can play *2 . . .* **R—K8ch;** *3* **QxR** (or *3* **K—B2, Q—K6 mate), QxQ** mate. Black's first move was an example of *removing the guard.*

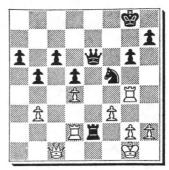

238B. Black moves. His Knight is attacked; hence *1 . . .* **Kt—KKt3,** parrying the threat. *But White had another threat,* made possible by the retreat of the Bishop. This menace, far from obvious, now becomes reality: *2* **Q—B8ch, BxQ;** *3* **RxB** mate! Black could have avoided this mate, but only at the cost of leaving his attacked Knight in the lurch.

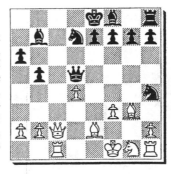

239B. White moves. He has only one reply, *3* **KxQ,** which is resoundingly answered by *3 . . .* **R—Q8** mate. Black's Pawn at KB6 acts as a powerful wedge (actually doing the work of a Bishop or Queen) in blocking the escape of the White King. All of Black's moves were violent: *the more stringently the defense is limited, the easier it is to foresee the consequences.*

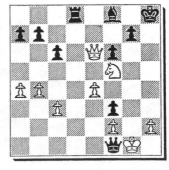

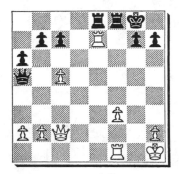

240A. White moves. He begins with *1* **Q—B4***ch* (*1* Q—Kt3*ch* has the same effect), which is as strong as it is obvious. Strong because it drives Black's King into the corner, *which makes his first rank vulnerable;* obvious because *all checks and captures are obvious*—they must be the first moves one looks at. Black is forced (why?) to play *1 . . .* **K—R1.** Now comes the brilliant *2* **Q—B7!**

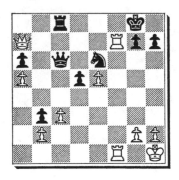

241A. White moves. He plans to drive Black's King into the corner. As in 240A, Black's King will have no mobility—no space to move freely if checked. *Knowing what to look for,* White plays the brilliant *1* **RxP***ch!* Black replies *1 . . .* **KtxR** (*1 . . .* K —R1 allows mate in two—how?). The play continues *2* **Q—B7***ch,* **K—R1.**

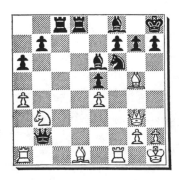

242A. White moves. He plays the "brilliant" move *1* **RxKt?,** reckoning on *1 . . .* PxR; *2* BxP*ch* and mate next move. But, by removing his Rook from the first rank, White has weakened that line. Black reasons that if the other Rook disappears, *the vulnerable first rank will be open to mating threats.* This leads to the forcing *1 . . .* **QxR!**

240B. Black moves. There is no adequate defense to the threat of *3 QxP mate.* If Black plays *3 . . . Rx Q; 4 RxRch* forcing mate next move on the vital rank. *3 . . .* R—KKt1 guards the mate, but *4 RxR* has catastrophic consequences for Black.

The chief cause of Black's downfall is the uselessness of his Queen. *Successful attack or efficient defense is difficult without the Queen.*

241B. White moves. His brilliant next move should be seen in a flash —*look for checks and captures!* Black's first rank, guarded only by a Rook, is attacked by White's Queen and Rook. How can this concentrated menace be utilized? Answer: *3 Q—B8 ch!, RxQ; 4 RxR* mate. Four consecutive checks, two of them captures, led to Black's downfall.

242B. White moves. Threatened with mate or disastrous loss of material, he is resigned to his fate. He plays *2 KtxQ,* allowing *2 . . . RxB ch* and mate in two more moves.

When the Rooks are disconnected, as in 242A, *there is often a likelihood that the first rank will be vulnerable to attack.*

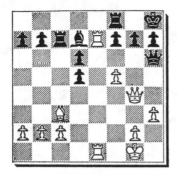

243A. White moves. He has two attacking "batteries": the Queen, Bishop and King Bishop Pawn operate against KKt7; the Rooks control the only open line. To obtain the cooperation of all these forces, he uses *a discovered attack*: *1* RxB!, Rx R; *2* P—B6! (This Pawn has been *unpinned* by the sacrifice of the exchange.)

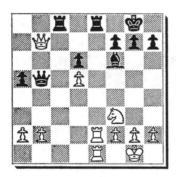

244A. Black moves. He must not snatch at the Queen: *1 . . .* QxQ*??; 2* RxR*ch*, RxR; *3* RxR mate—*vulnerable first rank!* Instead, Black plays the startling but logical *1 . . .* **QxR!** *making use of the same weapon to checkmate White!* After *2* **RxQ** White's first rank is vulnerable. Black proves this immediately as his Rook whizzes down the open file: *2 . . .* **R—B8***ch.*

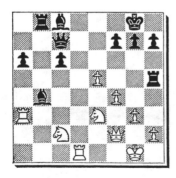

245A. White moves. His first observation is that Black's Rooks are disconnected—*always a likely indication of a weak first rank.* But White's goal is not mate; he sees that he can only force the win of a piece. After *1* **KtxB, RxKt;** *2* **Q—Q2** there is a double attack menacing the Rook at QKt5 and also threatening *3* Q—Q8*ch*, QxQ; *4* RxQ mate.

243B. Black moves. He is confronted with two threats: *3 QxR or 3 PxPch,* which wins at least a Rook. To parry both threats, he is forced to play *2 . . . R(B1)—Q1.* But White wins anyway: *3 QxR!* After *3 . . . R xQ* Black's first rank is denuded of defenders. He is helpless against the deadly Rook move: *4 R—K8* mate.

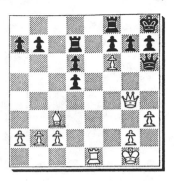

244B. White moves. He cannot stave off mate, but he has a venomous last trap. If he tries *3 R—K1,* then *3 . . . RxRch; 4 KtxR, RxKt* mate. Instead, White plays *3 Kt—K1,* inviting the blunder *3 . . . RxR??* when *4 Q —Kt8ch* (or *4 Q—R8ch*) *forces checkmate on Black!* But Black is wary: he plays *3 . . . RxKtch!; 4 RxR, RxR* mate. These witty possibilities deserve careful study.

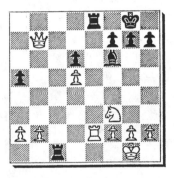

245B. Black moves. He realizes that if he retreats his Rook from attack, he will be mated as shown. So he defends both threats with *2 . . . Q—K2.* White plays *3 Q—Q8ch* just the same. He sees that he will win a piece. Black interposes with *3 . . . Q—B1* (not *3 . . . QxQ??; 4 RxQ* mate) and now White wins a piece with *4 QxQch, KxQ; 5 R—Q8ch* (double attack!).

QUIZ ON THE VULNERABLE FIRST RANK

246. White moves. *What is the quickest way to remove the guardian of Black's first rank, making the Black King vulnerable to mate next move?*

247. White moves. He cannot force mate, but he can make use of the *vulnerable first rank* idea to queen his Passed Pawn. How? (*Hint:* see 221B.)

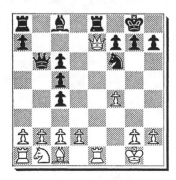

248. White moves. His situation is apparently critical, for if he plays *1 Q—Q6* (forced?) there follows *1 . . . RxRch; 2 K—B2, Kt—K5ch.* Yet White can win by exploiting Black's vulnerable first rank. How?

249. White moves. Black's Bishop is paralyzed and prevents the Rook from guarding the first rank. *How can White win material by taking advantage of the weakness of Black's first rank?*

(Solutions on pages 230–231)

16: BREAKING COMMUNI-CATION

Parting is such sweet sorrow—SHAKESPEARE
The dearest friends are separated by impassable gulfs—EMERSON
Examine moves that smite! A good eye for smites is far more important than a knowledge of strategical principles
—PURDY

WE HAVE SEEN how a piece which is attacked may be won, by making life miserable for its defender. The protector is either destroyed, removed by exchange, or driven off. In all such cases, the defensive function comes to an end.

When these methods of gentle persuasion fail, another effective device is still available. This is to interpose a piece (or force the enemy to do so!) which interferes with the flow of force leading from the piece under attack to its protector. The life-giving current is shut off; the threatened piece is stranded and left to its fate.

Pieces which do not have effective contact with their own forces (such as a Knight stranded at the edge of the board) are particularly susceptible to a break in communications. In general, beware of time-wasting captures which require a piece to travel far afield.

BASIC PATTERN FOR
BREAKING COMMUNICATION

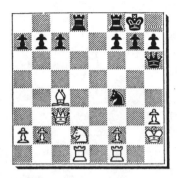

250A. **Black moves.** His powerful pressure against the King Rook Pawn is neutralized by White's Queen. Black breaks the line of communication by *1 . . . R—Q6!!*

250B. **White moves.** If he plays *2 BxR*, Black continues *2 . . . QxPch; 3 K—Kt1, Q—Kt7* mate. Or if *2 QxR, KtxQ; 3 Bx Kt, Q—Q3ch (double attack!)* and wins.

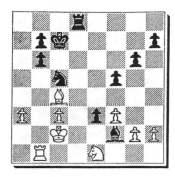

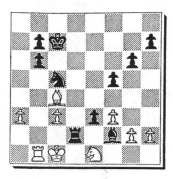

251A. Black moves. His Bishop attacks White's Knight, which is protected by his Rook. The Rook cannot be driven off, nor threatened with capture or exchange. *Yet its protective power can be nullified* by *1 . . . R—Q7ch,* forcing *2 K—B1.*

251B. Black moves. He still attacks the Knight, but it is no longer guarded by the Rook. *The line of communication has been snapped* by the forced retreat of White's King. Consequently Black wins easily by simply removing the Knight: *2 . . . BxKt.*

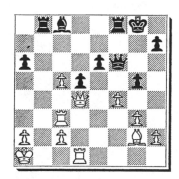

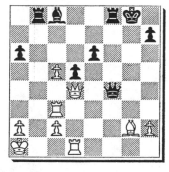

252A. Black moves. He plays to win a Pawn, without realizing that he will be breaking the line of communication that guards a vital piece. He captures by *1 . . . PxP* and after *2 PxP,* he snatches the seemingly undefended Pawn by *2 . . . QxP?*

252B. White moves. His Queen attacks Black's Queen, which is protected by a Rook. *He severs the line of communication* with *3 R—Kt3ch!* If now *3 . . . K—B2,* Black's Queen has lost the protection of the Rook, so that *4 QxQch* wins at once.

253A. White moves. He pins and doubly attacks Black's Bishop at K2, which is doubly defended. *To drive away Black's Queen from the defense,* White plays *1* **B—KB4.** Now Black cannot play *1 . . . QxB??* (*removal of the guard*) because of *2 QxB* mate. Or, if *1 . . . Q—KB3,* the *skewer 2 B—Kt5* makes the *pin* decisive. Black therefore tries *1 . . . Q—B4.*

253B. White moves. He plays *2 P—Q6,* striking for the third time at the pinned Bishop, which is overwhelmed, as it is attacked three times and defended only once. The Queen's Pawn has added its weight to the attack; but more important is the fact that it has wedged itself between Bishop and Queen, *cutting their line of communication.* Black is lost; if *2 . . . PxP; 3 Qx B* mate.

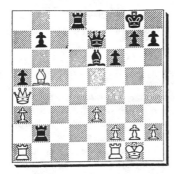

254A. Black moves. He can win a piece, but how? His Rook at Kt7 attacks the Bishop, which, however, is defended. How can Black break the line of communication *when there is no line of communication?!* The answer is: by creating such a line! Thus: *1 ... R—Q4.* White replies *2 B—K8,* for if *2 B—B4, P—QKt4* wins a piece by *double attack!* (Retreat by the Bishop to Q3 or K2 was of course impossible.)

Black has separated the Queen and Bishop, yet the Queen still exercises protection from QR4 to K8.

254B. Black moves. With the venomous Pawn push *2 ... P —QKt4,* he *breaks the line of communication,* attacking the Queen and winning the Bishop. Creating a line of communication in order to break it is a novel device! There is an analogy in the story of the preacher who was exhorting his congregation to repent, and save themselves from the lot of sinners in the Hereafter—where "There will be weeping and wailing and gnashing of teeth." "Suppose I have no teeth?" an old lady asked. "Teeth will be provided," was the preacher's quick reply.

17: THE SURPRISE MOVE

A man surprised is half-beaten—PROVERB
He hath as many tricks as a dancing bear—SWIFT
There is always
a comforting thought
in time of trouble when
it is not our trouble—DON MARQUIS
A combination composed of a sacrifice has a more imme-
diate effect . . . than another combination, because the
apparent senselessness of the sacrifice is a convincing proof
of the design of the player offering it—RETI
The appeal of combinative play to the average reader is
founded on the factor of surprise, often brought about by
unexpected sacrifice of material, and the greater this ele-
ment enters into a combination, the greater its attraction
—YATES AND WINTER

ON THE CHESSBOARD, surprise is nothing more than logic that packs a wallop. The impact of surprise thrills the perpetrator, pleases the kibitzer, crushes the victim.

Many years ago, the distinction was subtly established by the famous lexicographer who was caught (by his wife, of course) in the act of kissing the maid.

"Why, John!" his wife exclaimed, "I'm surprised!"

Even in this trying situation (which might be described as the basic pattern for the surprise move), the dictionary-compiler's training did not desert him.

"You're not surprised," he answered. *"I'm* surprised. *You're* astonished."

Chess is so prolific in the variety of combinations it produces that it may seem pointless to isolate a certain kind of move and call it a "surprise" move. We have already been taught to "expect the unexpected." No matter how brilliant a move may be, it cannot startle us *if it is also the logical move*—the move that conforms to the pattern of the combination we are seeking.

Yet there are times when a move is so wildly fantastic that it jolts us out of our seats—until we realize that for all its bizarre appearance, it is earnestly sane and carefully evaluated. Such a move, which ruthlessly rips away the superficial aspects of the position, may rightfully be called a "surprise" move.

For the audience witnessing a game between experts, a surprise move has the thrill an unexpected knockout gives to fight fans watching two evenly matched prize fighters. For the reader of master games, a surprise move gives more joy than seven miles of painfully correct analysis. The surprise move has all the delicious quality of a witty remark lighting up a learned discourse.

When do such moves occur? Usually at the beginning of a combination: a piece is given up to smash the hostile King's position by a mating attack. But often the surprise move can be played with incomparably greater effect as the last in a series of innocuous moves or exchanges, in a position which seems completely harmless.

This second course is a great favorite with the modern master, who finds it highly effective, because less hackneyed, to wind up his combination with a stinging surprise.

It may seem out of place to give advice on how to guard against surprise moves, when the greatest masters have at one time or another succumbed to their electrifying effect. *But the habit of examining every possible check or capture* will reduce your losses.

The positions which follow may be studied with profit, but their chief purpose is to delight the reader with their fireworks effects. As for the victims of surprise moves, they may agree with Caesar, who, when asked which sort of death was the best, said: "That which is unexpected."

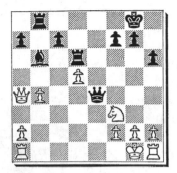

255A. **Black moves.** He invades enemy territory by *1 . . . Q—K7,* threatening *2 . . . BxP* mate or *2 . . . QxP* mate. It is relatively best for White to make a temporary escape with *2 P—KR3,* with a prosaic loss in prospect. But he instinctively guards the weak spot with *2 R—KB1?*

256A. **White moves.** He has given up a piece for a strong attack, which is all the more virulent because *Black's Queen is cut off from the defense.* For his concluding combination, he has prepared a charming sacrifice. He plays *1 B—Kt7ch* forcing *1 . . . K—B2.* And now the *surprise: 2 Q—K6ch!!*

257A. **White moves.** How can his Queen participate in the attack *with no loss of time?* To avoid giving Black a breathing spell, White plays *1 B—Kt5!* Black must do something about his Queen—*at once!* Therefore he has no time to attend to his King's welfare. Black replies *1 . . . QxB* (other Queen moves allow the same continuation).

255B. **Black moves.** He has a *surprise move*: 2 . . . **QxKt!!** White captures by 3 **PxQ**, whereupon Black gracefully winds up the White King's career with 3 . . . **R—Kt3** mate—an "epaulet" mate! The White Rooks which hover so anxiously around their King actually bring about his downfall!

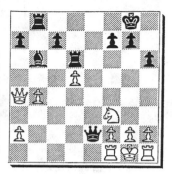

256B. **Black moves.** Rocked on his heels by the unexpected Queen sacrifice, he has no choice but to accept: 2 . . . **KtxQ.** The capture is answered by 3 **PxKt** mate! Despite the army of White pieces trained on Black's King, it remained for the not-so-humble Pawn to deal the death-blow!

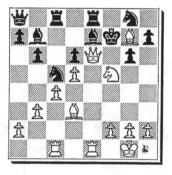

257B. **White moves.** His clever Bishop sacrifice cleared the way for action by the Queen—but not at once (2 **Q—R5??**, **Q—B8** mate!). Again time is of the essence—another *violent* move is needed: 2 **RxPch!**, forcing 2 . . . **KxR.** Now White mates by 3 **Q—R5ch,** **B—R3**; 4 **QxB** mate. *"Surprise is nothing more than logic that packs a wallop."*

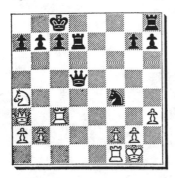

258A. White moves. Threatened with mate on the move, he hits on the superb surprise move *1 Kt—Kt6 ch!!* Pundits would analyze this fearless plunge into a nest of hostile Pawns as a Knight fork, based on a pin (*Black's Bishop Pawn is paralyzed*), plus a sacrifice as a clearance for the White Queen. But for our purposes the Knight move is a magnificent stroke, too delightful to desecrate by dissection!

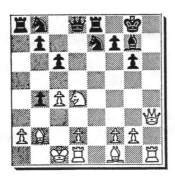

259A. Black moves. He sees the three-move threat of mate with *1 Q—R7ch, K—B1; 2 Kt—K6ch, PxKt; 3 QxB* mate. What more natural than *1 . . . BxKt* parrying the threat and winning a piece? But Black gets a rude awakening, as White replies with the electrifying *2 Q—R8ch!!*

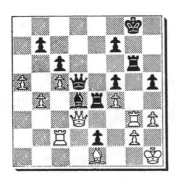

260A. Black moves. He plays *1 . . . R—K6.* This attacks the Queen. If *2 RxR(K3)??, QxP* mate. If White retreats his Queen from attack, then *2 . . . RxR; 3 BxR, RxB* with a piece ahead.

But White thinks he sees a way out: gaining time with a check, he will remove one of the Rooks and then pin the dangerous Queen: *2 RxRch, PxR; 3 Q—B4.*

258B. Black moves. He captures:
1 . . . PxKt. Utilizing the open Queen Rook file, White replies *2 Q—R8* mate. (Black could have avoided the mate by moving his King in reply to *1 Kt—Kt6ch!!*—but this would have meant losing the Queen.)

This is a perfect example of the value of *studying every possible check or capture.*

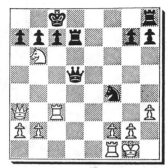

259B. Black moves. He has no
choice: he must play *2 . . . BxQ,* allowing *3 RxB* mate. The Queen sacrifice seems a lot less startling to one who is familiar with *mating patterns* (see the section on that subject). An early combination by Dr. Euwe, who later became World Champion.

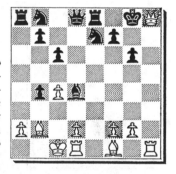

260B. Black moves. Apparently
White has defended with genuine skill. He has avoided the loss of a piece, and he is about to exchange Queens. True, Black can now win by *3 . . . QxQ; 4 RxQ, R—Q6* and *5 . . . R—Q8.* But at least White will be losing creditably.

Instead, Black mates on the move: *3 . . . RxP* mate! *The pinned Queen is still pinning!*

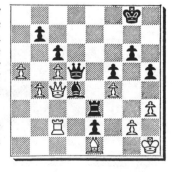

261A. White moves. He is the exchange ahead—enough to win, but there is no obvious immediate decision. However, White has a beautiful surprise move which gives Black his quietus: *1 R—Q5!!, offering his Rook in four different ways!* Despite these alternative ways of capturing, the White Rook is anything but vulnerable.

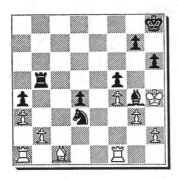

262A. Black moves. Since White's King cannot move, mate can be administered by any Black checking piece safe from capture. This is the logical explanation of the extraordinary play that follows: *1 . . . RxP!!* threatening *2 . . . RxP* mate. If now *2 P—R3, R—KR7* or if *2 R—R1, Kt —K8,* forcing mate in either case. White prefers to be "shown." He plays *2 BxR,* which is answered by the stunning *2 . . . Kt—K4!!*

263A. Black moves. He begins with *1 . . . RxB!* relying on a Knight fork (if *2 PxR?* the family check *2 . . . Kt—B6ch* wins at once). But White has a resource: counterattack with *2 R—QB5.*

Black (Marshall) plays *2 . . . Q— KKt6!!!* The Queen must be taken, as *3 . . . QxRP* mate is menaced.

261B. Black moves. Which way does he want to be mated? If *1 . . . QxR;* 2 **Q—B6** mate *(overworked Queen)*. If *1 . . . RxR;* 2 **Q—B8** mate *(vulnerable first rank)*. Finally, if *1 . . . PxR* or *1 . . . BxR;* 2 **QxR** mate *(breaking communications)!* Nor can Black really refuse the Rook, as 2 QxR mate and 2 RxQ are threatened.

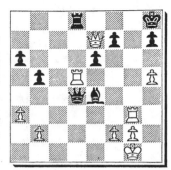

262B. White moves. Life is still very difficult for him, the threat being *3 . . . Kt—Kt3* mate! He has no alternative but to play *3* **PxKt.** But now the real blow descends, for Black's earlier sacrifices, brilliant though they were, served only as preliminaries. Black plays *3 . . .* **P—Kt4** mate! *It was the fatal position of the White King that made the surprise moves logical.*

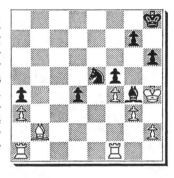

263B. White moves. *His opponent has just played the most brilliant move in the history of chess!* White is helpless: if *3* **RPxQ,** Kt—K7 mate! If *3* **BPxQ,** Kt—K7*ch;* *4* K—R1, RxR mate. Or *3* **QxQ,** Kt—K7*ch;* *4* K—R1, KtxQ*ch;* *5* K—Kt1, Kt—K7*ch* with a piece ahead. So White resigns. "Some of Marshall's most sparkling moves look at first like typographical errors" (Napier).

18: COMBINED OPERA-TIONS

The scheme of a game is played on positional lines; the decision of it, as a rule, is effected by combinations—RETI
The middle-game I repeat is chess itself; chess with all its possibilities, its attacks, defenses, sacrifices, etc.—ZNOSKO-BOROVSKY
In the perfect chess combination as in a first-rate short story, the whole plot and counter-plot should lead up to a striking finale, the interest not being allayed until the very last moment—YATES AND WINTER

THERE HAS NEVER BEEN a good definition of the word "combination." We can come close to the real meaning by saying that a combination is a series of forcing moves which result in checkmate, gain of material, or improvement in position. In a combination *we impose our will on the opponent by forcing his replies.*

The patterns that we have studied so far—the pin, the Knight fork, the double attack, the discovered check and the rest, are all fundamental; *they form the basis of combination play.*

When we combine two or more of these themes—say a pin followed by a Knight fork—we are on the way to understanding *and playing combinations* on a grand scale, the kind that mark the play of a master. Combinations which at first sight may seem difficult to understand, become clear and simple when broken down into their component parts. The amazing combinations of Alekhine, Keres, Capablanca and the other great masters *can be reduced to basic elements that we know and understand from our study of the preceding chapters.*

What these masters create on the chessboard may be compared appropriately to the full stage presentation of the master magician. The layman is bewildered by the overpowering procession of illusions. The magician's colleagues, on the other hand, see in his performance "nothing more" than a grand combination of familiar themes. The sleight-of-hand, the shuffling and concealment of cards, the palming of coins, the disappearing goldfish, the woman sawed in half—all these are only the equivalent of the chess master's bag of tricks: the pins, Knight forks, double attacks and discovered checks.

There is one important distinction between the magician and the chess master. When the layman discovers how illusions are created, there is a great psychological letdown. When the chess student is given a rational explanation of the mechanics of chess combination, his enjoyment of the game is intensified.

BASIC PATTERN FOR COMBINED OPERATIONS

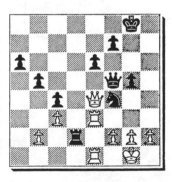

264. **Black moves.** He sees that *1 . . . Kt—R6ch* wins against all four possible replies: if *2 PxKt, QxPch; 3 K—R1, QxP* mate. If *2 RxKt, QxQ,* and White's *overworked Rook* cannot recapture; for if *3 RxQ, R—Q8ch* leads to mate on the *vulnerable first rank.* If *2 K—B1, RxP* mate or *2 . . . QxP* mate. Finally, if *2 K—R1, KtxPch* wins the Queen by a *Knight fork.*

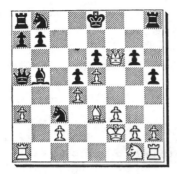

265A. Black moves. He sees an attractive *Knight fork* which threatens King and Queen: *1 . . . Kt—K5 ch.* But White has a Pawn guarding the crucial square! The unthinking player would discard the idea at this point; but one familiar with combination patterns looks further ahead. *He makes the impossible moves become possible!* Black plays *1 . . . Kt —K5ch!* forcing *2 PxKt.*

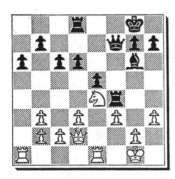

266A. White moves. Will it be giving away the plot to say that White wins material by a combination involving a *Knight fork* followed by a *pin?* The first link in the chain is an attack on Black's Queen: *1 Kt— Kt5.* (His object, improbable as it may *seem,* is to play *2 Kt—K6,* forking the Black Rooks.) Black replies *1 . . . Q—K1,* hoping to guard the vital square.

267A. White moves. He notes that the mobility of Black's Queen *is severely constricted.* How can White exploit this state of affairs? He looks for a violent move. *1 P—QKt4,* attacking the Queen and unpinning the Knight, answers the purpose. After the forced reply *1 . . . Q— Kt3,* White follows up with *2 KtxP,* this time forcing *2 . . . Q—B3.*

265B. **Black moves.** His opponent's King and Queen are in line, making possible a *pin* on the King Bishop file. *2 . . . R—B1* wins White's Queen.

Black has combined two familiar patterns, the Knight fork and the pin, to form his winning combination. Heaven-sent inspiration? No! *Black succeeded because he knew what to look for!*

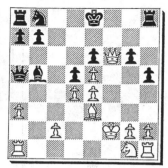

266B. **White moves.** His intended invasion is prevented, but only ostensibly so. As a combination player (one who is familiar with the basic winning patterns), White is not discouraged: he merely looks one move ahead and plays *2 Kt—K6!* menacing both Rooks. After *2 . . . QxKt* he plays *3 QxR!* exploiting the *pin* on Black's King Pawn. White has won the exchange.

267B. **White moves.** Should he retreat his attacked Knight? No, because he has a stronger move. Note that Black's King and Queen are in line. This makes a pin possible: *3 B —Kt5.* The pin works even though the Bishop is unguarded: *3 . . . Qx B* is answered by the picturesque family check *4 KtxPch* winning the Queen with an easy win.

268A. White moves. He has given up two Pawns to reach this promising combinative position. After *1* **KtxB, PxKt** he can regain one of the lost Pawns by *2* **Kt—B4,** attacking the Queen and King's Pawn. But this pedestrian continuation is not good enough. *After studying every check and capture,* he plays *2* **RxPch!**

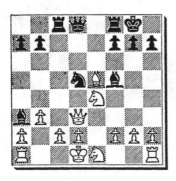

269A. Black moves. White's centrally posted Bishop and Knight are *insecure,* as they are not guarded by Pawns. This calls for the powerful but fairly obvious *1 . . .* **R—K1,** striking at the Bishop and the pinned Knight behind it. *2* **P—KB4** is now forced, and play continues *2 . . .* **B xKt,** this time forcing *3* **QxB.**

270A. White moves. In the most innocent-looking positions, there often lurk deadly but delightful combinations. Who would suspect that White can impale his opponent's King and Queen by a *pin,* or run them through with a *skewer?* To combine these motifs—that is the art of chess. *1* **Q—Q8***ch* forces *1 . . .* **K—B2;** now *2* **P—K6***ch!* is decisive.

268B. **Black moves.** His King and Queen are attacked by the impudent, unprotected Rook, which must be captured. In the words of the Queen of Hearts, "Off with his head!" Black plays 2 ... QxR. But now White trumps this trick with 3 KtxPch, an attractive Knight fork which wins the Queen.

269B. **Black moves.** White's pinned Knight has disappeared, but his pinned Bishop is now the target. If 3 ... P—B3 White escapes by counterattack (*1* Q—R4). *Study every check and capture!* This yields the brilliant solution 3 ... Kt—B6ch! forking King and Queen. *4* PxKt is impossible; *4* BxKt loses White's Queen.

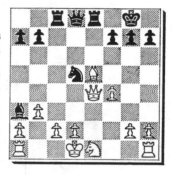

270B. **Black moves.** He must capture the fatal Pawn, and either method of capture allows a pretty conclusion. Thus if 2 ... KxP; 3 Q —K8ch wins Black's Queen by the skewer. Or if 2 ... QxPch the newly unpinned Bishop asserts his freedom with the malevolent 3 B—B4, pinning (and winning) Black's Queen. A deceptively simple position!

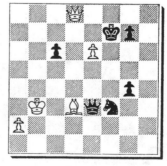

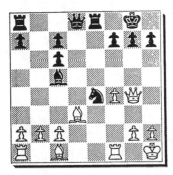

271A. **Black moves.** He wins a piece by combining three different ideas: Queen sacrifice, Knight fork and vulnerable first rank. This is all less formidable than it sounds. To begin with, he is dissatisfied with *1 . . . Kt—B7ch; 2 RxKt, BxR* which merely wins the exchange. If only *2 . . . R—K8ch* were feasible! But White can interpose at B1. The solution: *1 . . . QxB!!; 2 PxQ.*

272A. **White moves.** Broken down into cold technical terms, his delightful combination makes use of a Queen sacrifice to seize the *vulnerable last rank*. There he pins a defended piece. Another pin, based on a sacrifice, *removes the guard*. Awe-inspiring as this may sound, the themes are old friends by now:

1 QxKt!	**PxQ**
2 RxRch	**B—K1**

273A. **White moves.** Zukertort, who had the White pieces here, was a "sugar-cake" in name only! He begins with the amazing Queen sacrifice *1 Q—Kt5!* The reply *1 . . . Qx Q* is unavoidable, for if *1 . . . K— Q2?; 2 P—B8(Q)ch* or *2 QxQch* leaves White a Queen ahead. The combination unfolds with *2 P—B8(Q)ch, K— B2* (if *2 . . . Kt—Q1?* the Knight fork *3 Kt—B7ch* wins the Queen).

271B. **Black moves.** Now the combination clicks. He plays 2 . . . **Kt—B7***ch*. White dare not take the Knight, for then *3* . . . R—K8*ch* forces mate (his Rook-protecting Bishop has disappeared from Q3!). So *3* **K—Kt1** must be played, whereupon *3* . . . **Kt**x**Q***ch* leaves Black a piece to the good.

The different combinative motifs have been smoothly blended.

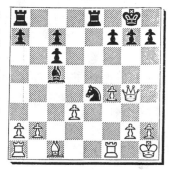

272B. **White moves.** He must remove the guard of the pinned Bishop before Black can consolidate his defense. Therefore *3* **BxP** pinning the Queen. Black is lost. He must play *3* . . . **QxB**, else he loses the Queen. But now that the guard is removed, White plays *4* **RxB** mate.

Again we must admire the slick interplay of several combinative motifs.

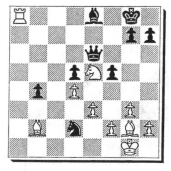

273B. **White moves.** His next two moves should be seen in a flash by conscientious students of combination patterns. What can White obtain in return for parting with the precious Passed Pawn? The answer: *3* **QxKt***ch!*, **KxQ** and now the Knight fork *4* **Kt—B7***ch* wins Black's Queen. The upshot of the ingenious combination is that White has won a piece *by forcing moves.*

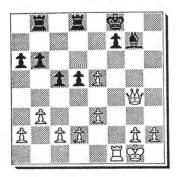

274A. White moves. His material advantage is enough to win, but he wants victory by the quickest route. Therefore he seeks *forcing* moves. The indicated target is Black's King Bishop Pawn, which is on an open file. So White begins with *1 P—K6.* Black defends with *1 . . . R—Kt2* and White adds more weight to the pin with *2 Q—Kt6,* forcing *2 . . . P—B3.*

275A. Black moves. His combination hinges on the fact that the two Queens are *en prise* to each other. He begins with a brutal move (and in chess one must be brutal):

1	RxKt*ch!*
2 RxR	RxR*ch*
3 KxR	. . . .

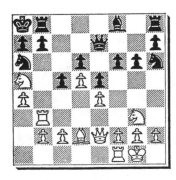

276A. White moves. The beautifully intermeshed combination which follows is based on the fact that Black's Bishop has to guard a Knight and the Queen *(overworked piece!),* and on the lack of communication between Black's Rooks. Throughout, we *seek checks and captures:*

1 QxKt!!	PxQ
2 RxR*ch*	KxR
3 Kt—B6*ch*	. . . .

274B. White moves. Again on the lookout for *violent* moves, he breaks through with a sacrifice: *3* **Rx Pch!, BxR** (if *3* . . . K—Kt1; *4* R—B7 is decisive). After *4* **QxBch** Black must play *4* . . . **K—K1** to guard his Rook at Q1 from the double attack of White's Queen. Now White winds up with a skewer: *5* **Q—R8ch, K—K2;** *6* **Q—Kt7ch** (or *6* **Q—R7ch**) winning the Rook at Kt2.

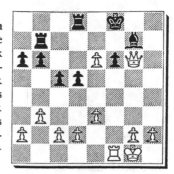

275B. Black moves. Now for the pretty point of the combination: *3* . . . **Kt—B6ch!,** forking King and Queen. If White moves his King, then *4* . . . **KtxQ.** If instead *4* **RxKt** (overworked Rook!), then *4* . . . **Qx Qch.** In either event, White's Queen is lost, and with it the game.

276B. Black moves. He answers the Knight fork with *3* . . . **K—Kt2.** The obvious sequel is *4* **KtxQ.** White is now a piece ahead! For if *4* . . . **B xKt,** the Knight at R3 loses its protection, allowing *5* **BxKt.** If White's Knight at K7 is not captured, it makes its escape to QB6.

This lone example is a veritable treatise on combination play.

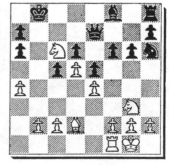

277A. Black moves. His enormous advantage in position (based on the *indirect pin* by the Bishop) more than outweighs his material disadvantage. But to translate this into quick victory, he needs forcing moves. He begins with *1 . . . QxP!* If the Queen is captured (*vulnerable first rank*), *2 . . . R—B8* mate.

277B. White moves. He plays *2 R—K1* (if *2 R—KKt1*, Black has two ways of mating in two moves—how?). Black insists on sacrificing his Queen by *2 . . . QxKtch!* Then if *3 KxQ, R—B7* with double check and mate. Equally pretty is *3 RxQ, R—B8* mate. Being pinned, White's Rook must stay at K2.

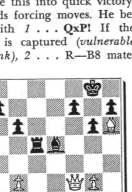

278A. White moves. The Black Bishop is *pinned!* Hence the artistic move *1 Q—B6!* Black must not play *1 . . . BxQ* because of *2 R—K8* mate. So he tries *1 . . . QxBP*, giving the Bishop more protection.

278B. White moves. Still searching for *violent* methods, he plays the exquisite sequel *2 Q—Kt7ch!!* Black must play *2 . . . BxQ*, clearing the King file. This permits *3 R—K8ch, B—B1; 4 RxB* mate!

QUIZ ON COMBINED OPERATIONS

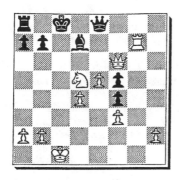

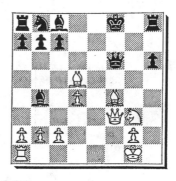

279. White moves. He has several ways of winning, but the quickest is based on a *pin* followed by a *Knight fork*. How would you demonstrate this?

280. White moves. His *modus operandi* is a *discovered attack* followed by a *Knight fork*. What two moves does he play to bring this about?

281. White moves. He can win material by means of a *double attack*, followed by a *pin*. How?

282. White moves. Creating a *pin* allows him to win by *double attack on the following move*. How?

(Solutions on page 231)

19: DESIGN FOR CHECK-MATE

*A thorough understanding of the typical mating continuations makes the most complicated sacrificial combinations leading up to them not only not difficult, but almost a matter of course—*TARRASCH

*As soon as a true thought has entered our mind, it gives a light which makes us see a crowd of other objects which we have never perceived before—*CHATEAUBRIAND

Look at Legal's mate. The mediocre chess player will never invent anything like it . . . but when the mechanism of the stratagem has been explained to him, this same player will be able not only to reproduce it when occasion arises, but to apply it in other positions—*ZNOSKO-BOROVSKY

THE MATING PATTERNS which follow have been chosen for their practical value. They are repetitive, standard, effective.

The chess pieces, with their differentiated powers of movement and capture, may be manipulated with such artistry as to produce the most exquisite combinations. These "things of beauty" delight our aesthetic sense so keenly that we are apt to forget *the means by which the combination was produced.* The situation needs analysis:

We are thrilled when a player brushes aside all the superfluities and irrelevancies of a position with his brilliant sacrifices. But on sober second thought, we realize that he can be so scintillating because he has an eye—call it an x-ray eye—which pierces through to the very skeleton of the mating pattern.

* A brief example of the Legal mate: *1* P—K4, P—K4; *2* B—B4, P—Q3; *3* Kt—KB3, B—Kt5; *4* Kt—B3, P—KR3; *5* KtxP!, BxQ; *6* BxP*ch*, K—K2; *7* Kt—Q5 mate!

As you study Diagrams 283–295, you may be troubled by the fact that White's King is almost always lacking and that there is a great disparity in material. The White King has been omitted because he is not needed for the skeleton mating process. The material on both sides has been removed in order to strip the positions of non-essentials.

In these diagrams, we are studying forms, patterns, basic set-ups. The diagrams are not intended to represent actual, concrete positions. Beginning with Diagram 296, we return to real positions from actual play—positions which show how the mating patterns are used by skilful players.

SKELETON PATTERN FOR A MATING COMBINATION

283A. White moves. He wants to break through *the barrier of Pawns*. The indicated target is the Knight's Pawn. It is guarded by the King, but *1 P—B6* menaces *2 QxP mate*. Black's Knight Pawn is pinned; hence his only defense is *1 . . . P—Kt3*. But this resource—the only one Black has, to be sure—will prove a flimsy one.

283B. White moves. He has accomplished his object: by advancing his Pawn, he has created a powerful wedge in Black's position. KKt7 is still the critical square. White proves this by playing *2 Q—R6*, after which *3 Q—Kt7* mate cannot be stopped. *This is a mating pattern*: see Diagram 289, which illustrates a similar mating pattern.

BASIC MATING PATTERNS

284. White moves. Queen, supported by Bishop, mates at KR7.

285. Queen, supported by Pawn wedge at KKt6, mates at KR7.

286. White moves. Queen, supported by Rook, mates on the open file.

287. White moves. Queen, supported by Knight, **mates at KR7.**

288. White moves. Queen, supported by Knight, **mates at KKt7.**

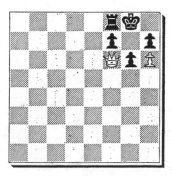

289. White moves. Queen, supported by Pawn wedge at KR6, **mates at KKt7.** Position of Queen and Pawn is often transposed.

290. White moves. Queen, supported by Bishop on KB6, mates at KKt7. Position of Queen and Bishop is often transposed.

291. White moves. Queen, supported by Bishop on the long diagonal, mates at KKt7 or KR8.

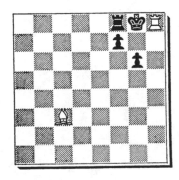

292. Rook (or Queen) supported by Bishop on the long diagonal, mates at KR8.

293. Rook, supported by Knight at KB6, mates at **KR7** or **KKt8**.

294. White moves. Doubled Rooks force mate on the seventh rank.

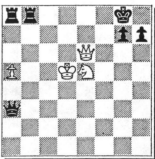

295. Black moves. Classic position for smothered mate by Queen and Knight. (From a book by Lucena published in 1496!) The winning process after *1* . . . K—R1 is *2* Kt—B7*ch*, K—Kt1; *3* Kt—R6*ch*, K—R1; *4* Q—Kt8*ch!!*, RxQ; *5* Kt—B7 mate!

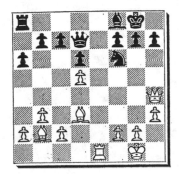

296A. White moves. All his pieces are trained on Black's Kingside. We see a mating pattern in the attack of Queen and Bishop against KR7 (*see Diagram 284*). For the time being, this target is guarded by Black's Knight. *Therefore the Knight must be removed*:

1 **BxKt**   **PxB**

297A. White moves. He has an overwhelming attack, based partly on the fact that Black has moved the Pawns in front of his King. This weakness, plus the concentration of White's forces, promises forceful sacrificial brilliancies to come. White's Queen is attacked. Instead of retreating the Queen, *he relies on the mating pattern of Diagram 292*. There follows *1* BxKt! Realizing that *1* . . . BxB; 2 QxRP is quite hopeless, Black tries *1* . . . **PxQ.**

298A. Black moves. His doubled Rooks are very powerful on the seventh rank. Were it not for the protective influence of the White Rook at KKt4, Black might be able to apply *the mating pattern of Diagram 294*. This automatically suggests a brilliant sacrifice: *1* . . . **Qx R!;** 2 **PxQ.**

296B. White moves. With the removal of the defending Knight, *White has secured the mating pattern he wanted.*

White now checkmates according to plan: *2 QxP* mate. This is a simple example (easy to understand and just as easy to apply) of the usefulness of being familiar with mating patterns.

297B. White moves. He must now prove the soundness of his Queen sacrifice. How? His Rook has a vital open file and is supported powerfully by the Bishop on KB6. White plays *2 RxBch*, which is answered by *2 . . . K—B1* (if *2 . . . K —R1; 3 R—Kt5* or *3 R—Kt4* or *3 R —Kt3* mate—the other Bishop also plays a role!). Now we are ready for the pattern of Diagram 292: *3 R—R7!* No squirming can stop *R—R8* mate.

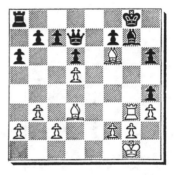

298B. Black moves. Having removed the defender of the seventh rank, Black carries out his plan:

2	RxPch
3 K—R1	R—R7ch
4 K—Kt1	R(QR7)—Kt7
	mate

This pattern has great practical value.

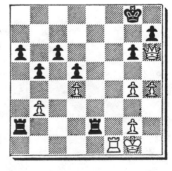

299A. White moves. "White's Knight is strongly posted at KB5." This comment, so often seen in annotations, introduces us to *the pattern of Diagram 288*. At this advanced post, the Knight offers ideal support for a checkmate with the Queen at KKt7. How is White's Queen to get access to the vital square without loss of time? White plays *1 Q—R6!* discounting the fact that he leaves his Rook unguarded.

300A. White moves. The situation of his attacking forces (Knight on KB6 and heavy pieces on the King Rook and King Knight files) reminds us irresistibly of *the pattern shown on Diagram 293*. The theoretically possible mates on KR7 or KKt8 are both prevented by Black's Rook at KKt2. The word *both* suggests that the Rook is *overworked.* And so it is: *1 QxPch!, RxQ.*

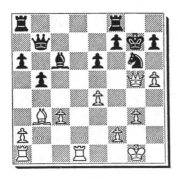

301A. White moves. He has sacrificed a piece, and can regain it if he wishes by *1 PxKt.* But he seeks a more forceful line. The position calls to mind *the pattern of Diagram 289*. Accordingly White plays *1 P—R6ch!* renouncing the regain of the piece. The Pawn wedge establishes a powerful bind on the adverse King's position.

299B. **Black moves.** As he cannot guard his KKt2, he snaps up the unprotected Rook. But after *1 . . . Qx R*ch*; 2 B—B1*, we perceive that the fate of the Rook was of no importance. What matters is that White, following the pattern for such positions, threatens *3 Q—Kt7* mate. To prevent this mate, Black would have to give up his Queen with *2 . . . Q —K6*ch*—a fatal loss of material.

300B. **White moves.** By sacrificing his Queen, White has created the desired mating position, and he winds up with *2 R—Kt8* mate.

White's sacrifice was brilliant; it was also logical. *Loss of material is of no consequence if a mating pattern can be attained;* such a pattern, plus the appropriate technique (in this case, the overworked piece) produces brilliant play.

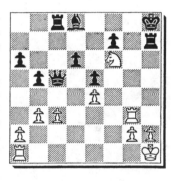

301B. **Black moves.** He gets out of check by *1 . . . K—Kt1*. Now comes *2 Q—B6* and Black is helpless against *3 Q—Kt7* mate. (The same position results from *1 . . . K—R1; 2 Q—B6*ch* etc.) In all these examples, the Queen is able to force mate at close range, supported by piece or Pawn. *The hostile King cannot touch a piece that is protected.*

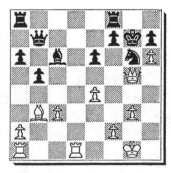

302A. Black moves. The sweeping diagonal of his Bishop on Kt2 suggests *the pattern of Diagram 292* —all the more so as Black has an open King Rook file. *1 . . . Q—R3* is too slow because of 2 P—KB3, defending KR2 and also closing the long diagonal. A *violent* move is needed: *1 . . . RxP!*

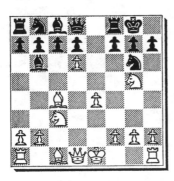

303A. White moves. He plays *1 Q—R5*, threatening 2 QxP mate *as in Diagram 287*. Remember that *the King is absolutely helpless to touch a piece which is protected*. Black must play *1 . . . P—KR3* to prevent the mate. After *2 QxKt* White again threatens mate at KR7. White's Queen is immune from capture, as Black's King Bishop Pawn is pinned. Hence *2 . . . PxKt* must be played.

304A. White moves. His Pawn at KKt6 reminds us of *the mating pattern of Diagram 285*. This calls for bringing the Queen to KR7; but White's Rooks are in the way, and he is also threatened with mate. He looks for *violent* moves:

1 R—R1*ch*	**K—Kt1**
2 R—R8*ch!*	**KxR**
3 R—R1*ch*	**K—Kt1**
4 R—R8*ch!*	**. . . .**

302B. White moves. He is threatened with 2 . . . R—R8 mate, *as per pattern.* White no longer has the defense 2 P—KB3, for this would allow 2 . . . RxQ. White plays 2 KxR and after 2 . . . Q—R3*ch* (2 . . . R—R1 *ch* also works); 3 K—Kt1 there follows 3 . . . Q—R8 mate. Applying the proper pattern made the Rook sacrifice a routine affair.

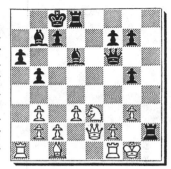

303B. White moves. His attempt to apply *the pattern of Diagram 287* has been foiled. But there are other patterns! He plays 3 BxP, and the momentary threat against the Black Queen gains time for the attack. After 3 . . . Q—K1 White plays 4 B —B6! with a beautiful double pin. The wedge with the Bishop forces mate (*see the pattern of Diagram 290*). Black's pieces are paralyzed by pins.

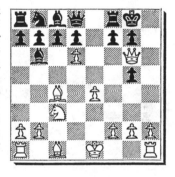

304B. Black moves. These Rook sacrifices are becoming monotonous! Black must again capture, but after 4 . . . KxR, the *pattern of the desired mate* has emerged in clear-cut form: 5 Q—R1*ch,* K—Kt1; 6 Q—R7 mate. To complete his design for checkmate, White did not shrink from sacrificing two Rooks. His knowledge of the pattern he needed guided him to a victorious conclusion.

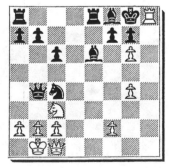

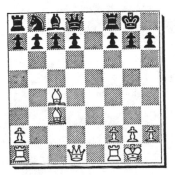

305A. White moves. Note how menacingly his Bishops are directed at Black's King-side. Black's Achilles heel is his KKt2, as White demonstrates with *1 Q—Kt4*. (*1 Q—Q4* looks more natural, but allows Black to defend with . . . Q—Kt4). Black is now embarrassed for a defense to the threatened mate, as he cannot play *1* . . . P—KB3 (the Pawn is pinned!) nor can he play *1* . . . Q—B3.

306A. White moves. He has three pieces trained on Black's Kingside. If he retreats his attacked Bishop, Black will have time to consolidate the defense. *Aiming for the pattern of Diagram 287,* White plays *1 BxPch!* Black replies *1* . . . KxB. (Evasion by *1* . . . K—R1 is pointless because of *2 Q—R5.*)

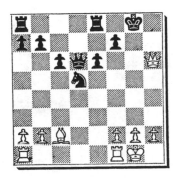

307A. White moves. The powerful position of his Queen and Bishop suggests *the mating pattern of Diagram 284.* But White must play the most exact moves. Thus *1 Q—R7ch?,* K—B1; *2 Q—R8ch* would allow Black to escape! The right way: *1 B—R7ch!,* K—R1. Black's King awaits his doom.

305B. **Black moves.** Reluctantly but unavoidably, he defends with *1 . . . P—KKt3*. Reluctantly, because of familiarity with *the mating pattern of Diagram 291*. But White also knows this mating pattern, and he continues *2 Q—Q4*, threatening *3 Q —Kt7* or *3 Q—R8* mate. With so many pieces still on the board, Black cannot prevent the threatened mate. (Remember that his King's Bishop Pawn is pinned and paralyzed!)

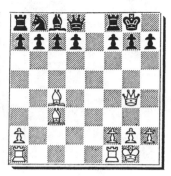

306B. **White moves.** He follows the pattern: *2 Q—R5ch, K—Kt1; 3 Kt—Kt5* threatening *4 Q—R7* mate. As *3 . . . QxKt* would leave him hopelessly behind in material, Black prepares for flight with *3 . . . R— Q1*. But "there ain't no hidin' place." White winds up with *4 Q—R7ch, K —B1; 5 Q—R8* mate. Another instance of the Queen's powers.

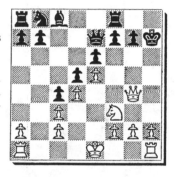

307B. **White moves.** He has forced Black's King to a square which is ideal for the hit-and-hold trick. Next comes *a discovered check*, but there is only one correct one! To wit: *2 B—Kt6ch!* The rest is easy: *2 . . . K—Kt1; 3 Q—R7ch, K—B1; 4 QxP* mate. (Why did the Bishop go to Kt6 on the second move?!)

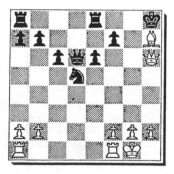

308A. White moves. *The pattern called for comes from Diagram 295. It is both pretty and picturesque, and has the added attraction of being of practical value. 1 Q—Q5ch forces 1 . . . K—R1 (if 1 . . . K—B1; 2 Q—B7 mate).*

308B. White moves. Now comes 2 Kt—B7ch, K—Kt1; 3 Kt—R6ch forcing 3 . . . K—R1. Now we are ready for *the smothered mate.* The sensational *4 Q—Kt8ch!* forces *4 . . . RxQ;* and now *5 Kt—B7* mate!

309A. Black moves. *He uses one mating pattern (Diagram 287) to bring about another (Diagram 286). 1 . . . Kt—KKt5* threatens *2 . . . QxP* mate. White defends with *2 PxKt* (not 2 R—K1, QxPch; 3 K—B1, QxP mate). But after *2 . . . PxP* Black has a new mate threat.

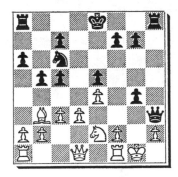

309B. White moves. The critical mating square cannot be guarded, so White decides to give the King elbow room. But after *3 R—K1, QxPch; 4 K—B1, Q—R6ch!!* (*4 . . . Q—R8ch?* would be inexact because of *5 Kt—Kt1*) forces *5 K—Kt1* permitting *5 . . . Q—R8* mate.

QUIZ ON DESIGNS FOR CHECKMATE

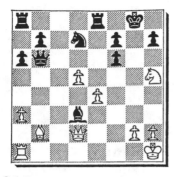

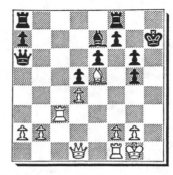

310. White moves. His advanced Knight at KR5 is a wonderful support for a mating pattern, with the Queen mating at KKt7. *What is the quickest way for White to bring about the mate?*

311. White moves. Working in harmony, his Rook at QB3 and his Bishop at K5 can combine to form a mating pattern. *How does White use them to force mate in two moves?*

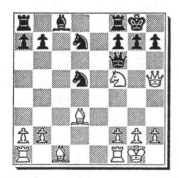

312. White moves. His Queen and Bishop are in line to threaten mate at KR7; but his own Knight stands in the way of the Bishop. *How does White get rid of the Knight, forcing mate in two moves?*

313. White moves. He can win Black's Queen by *1 R— R7ch*. But there is a quicker win: a mate in two moves, utilizing a mating pattern on the open Rook file. *How is this done?*

(Solutions on page 231)

20: THE MANLY ART OF SELF-DEFENSE

What boots it at one gate to make defense and at another to let in the foe?—MILTON
A man does not die of threats—PROVERB

AS YOUNGSTERS, we prefer being robbers to cops (a taste that some people never outgrow). Football heroes dream of 80-yard runs for a touchdown, leaving the dirty work of tackling to their comrades. Outfielders would much rather bat than field. In bridge, we all want to play the hand. Who would hesitate a moment between being a movie star or a movie extra?!

In chess, we find no exception to this universal desire to do what is glamorous, to engage in the activity that gives us a sense of power and the opportunity to be creative. Almost every chessplayer loves the attack, loathes the defense.

This attitude is quite natural. In attacking, we have a positive goal and we experience the artist's joy in devising ways to achieve our objective. If we encounter obstacles, that only adds zest to the problem. If our opponent puts up a good fight, so much the worse for him! *The main thing is that attack gives us freedom of action and the opportunity to choose.*

Defense, on the other hand, seems negative and artificial. It hampers us with restraints and subjects us to someone else's will. *It is our opponent* who attacks, dictates our replies, presses us unmercifully, keeps us preoccupied with the never-ceasing worry: "What's he up to now?"

Yet there are many things to be said in favor of cultivating your defensive ability. Defense is an integral part of the game: attack and defense are Siamese twins. So, whether we like it or not, we must reconcile ourselves to the need for skilful defensive play. When Carlyle was informed that Margaret Fuller had accepted the universe, he growled, "Gad, she'd better!" A poor defensive player is a poor chessplayer.

To cultivate our defensive skill means to cultivate useful qualities: skepticism, patience, resourcefulness, equanimity. When a poor defensive player meets unexpected difficulties, he either flies into a rage or goes to pieces. The clever defensive player confronts difficulties with a certain philosophic detachment and a grim determination to make the best of it. He not only gets better results; he gets more fun out of the game.

BASIC PATTERN FOR DEFENSIVE PLAY

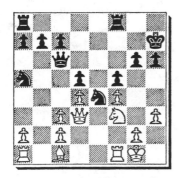

314A. White moves. His Pawn at QB3 is attacked twice, defended only once. White "disregards" the attack because he sees an *indirect* defense.

1 Kt—K5	QxP?
2 QxQ	KtxQ
3 B—Q2!	. . . .

314B. Black moves. He has won the Pawn in haste and can repent at leisure. As the Bishop skewers both Knights, the only try left for Black is *3 . . .* Kt—K7ch. But after *4* K—B2 both Knights are still attacked, and only one of them can be saved. This is an example of the theme *Don't Grab!*

DEFENSE TO A COMBINATION

315A. Black moves. He should retreat his Queen, which is attacked by the White Knight at KB3. Instead of retreating, Black plays to win the exchange. He succeeds in this, but loses the game *because he fails to look ahead one more move*:

1	B—B4*ch*
2 K—R1	Kt—B7*ch*
3 RxKt	. . . .

(Forced—why?)

315B. Black moves. He continues *3 . . . QxR* (of course not *3 . . . BxR*, as his Queen is attacked). Now White plays his ace in the hole: *4 Kt—K4!* Black's Queen is trapped, and has no way of returning to safety!

Thus we see that Black's combination proved fatal because it "succeeded." The operation was a success, but the patient died. In 316A we encounter a similarly faulty combination.

316A. White moves. He decides to sacrifice his Bishop at Q3 for three Pawns. His idea is to denude the Black King of Pawn protection. White begins with *1 BxP*, anticipating *1 . . . P—Kt3* (leaving the Bishop *no retreat*); *2 BxP, PxB; 3 QxP* with a good attack. But Black finds a subtle defense: *1 . . . BxKt!; 2 PxB, P—Kt3.*

316B. White moves. He proceeds with his plan: *3 BxP, PxB; 4 QxP?* At this instructive moment we can see why Black played *1 . . . BxKt!* For with that move he opened the King Knight file, with the result that White's King and Queen *are now in line on an open file.* A *pin* is called for: *4 . . . R—KKt1* pins —and wins—White's Queen!

317A. White moves. He relies on a pin, and Black "falls" for the combination:

1 RxP?	RxR!
2 QxR	PxQ
3 RxQ	. . . .

By means of this "clever" series of exchanges, White has won a Pawn.

317B. Black moves. His refutation takes the form of a queening threat: *3* . . . **P—B7!** *4* R—Q1 is answered by *4* . . . PxR(Q). *4* R—QB5 is answered by *4* . . . KtxR. *4* R—Q8*ch* (in order to play *5* R—QB8) is impossible because of *4* . . . KtxR. The Knight is truly "monarch of all he surveys."

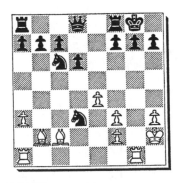

318A. White moves. The subtle opening move *1* **R—KKt1!** permits *1* . . . **BxKtP?!** and White "bites" with *2* **BxB!!** allowing *2* . . . **Kt—B5***ch*; *3* **K—R2, KtxQ.** Black is a full Queen ahead!

318B. White moves. *4* **Rx** **P***ch* forces *4* . . . **K—R1.** White has any number of *discovered checks,* but he knows that a *double check* is much more painful. So: *5* **R—Kt8***ch*!!, **KxR**; *6* **R—** **Kt1***ch*, **Q—Kt4**; *7* **RxQ** mate.

DON'T GRAB!

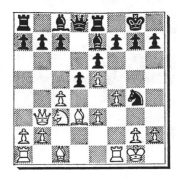

319A. Black moves. His Knight is badly out of play, with little prospect of reaching a better post. He sees what looks like a good opportunity of getting rid of the Knight and then regaining the piece by a *double attack*.

1	KtxKP(6)?
2 BxKt	P—Q5
3 QR—Q1!	....

A subtle resource. How does this refute Black's combination?

319B. Black moves. He must take Bishop or Knight (else he remains a piece down). Whichever way he captures, he *opens the Queen file*. This creates a familiar picture: *the pattern for discovered attack!* 4 . . . PxKt or 4 . . . PxB is answered by 5 Bx P*ch*, uncovering an attack on the Black Queen. After Black's King moves, 6 RxQ wins easily. White's calculations were simple: Black's moves were *forced*.

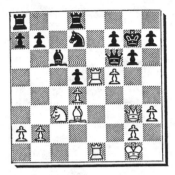 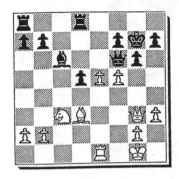

320A. Black moves. His Knight attacks White's Rook at K5. He grabs it by *1 . . . KtxR?* Thus he snatches at the opportunity of winning the exchange, *without taking the precaution of trying to discover White's defense to the threat.* White calmly recaptures by *2 PxKt.* The new Pawn at K5 menaces the Black Queen, which is sadly hampered by lack of *lebensraum.* This awkward situation should have been foreseen by Black.

320B. Black moves. His Queen has only one flight square, and he is forced to play *2 . . . Q—K2.* The reply *3 P—B6ch* is a devastating *double attack* on Black's King and Queen. White wins at once!

Black paid a high price for disregarding the maxim *"Don't grab!"* You cannot consider your opponent guilty of a blunder until you have carefully examined the resulting possibilities.

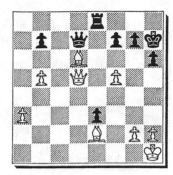

321A. **White moves.** Ostensibly he can win two pieces for a Rook—a clear material gain. Is there a catch? White sees no danger and grabs! After *1 RxB?*, *KtxR*; *2 QxKt* we have a position which illustrates the most familiar of all familiar themes: *the pin!*

321B. **Black moves.** His defense is predicated on the fact that the White Bishop on Q6 is *pinned and therefore paralyzed*. The approved procedure against the *pinned piece* is, *hit it again!* *2 . . . R—Q1* increases the pressure, forces the win of the Bishop with the exchange ahead.

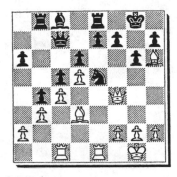

322A. Black moves. What could be more tempting than capturing the Bishop, forking Queen and both Rooks at the same time?! The temptation is irresistible: Black pounces on the Bishop with *1 . . . KtxB?* The reply is electrifying!

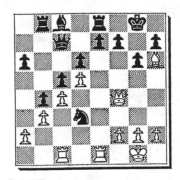

322B. White moves. He plays 2 **Q—B6!!** threatening *3* Q —Kt7 mate. (The position of the Bishop on KR6 was a clue to *the mating pattern of Diagram 290*.) Black plays 2 . . . **PxQ;** but then comes *3* **RxR** mate (*vulnerable first rank!*).

DEFENSE TO A THREAT

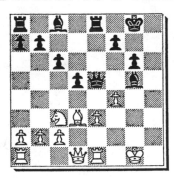

323A. Black moves. His Queen and Bishop are menaced by a Pawn fork: he must lose a piece. "Counterattack is the best defense," so: *1 . . .* **Q—Q3;** *2* **PxB** and now Black swoops down with a powerful check: *2 . . .* **Q—Kt6ch.**

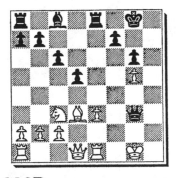

323B. White moves. His King is in a bad way. If *3* K—R1, K—Kt2! is decisive (threat: *4 . . .* R—R1ch). White tries *3* K —B1, but after *3 . . .* **B—R6ch;** *4* K—K2, **Q—Kt7** mate ends the King's agony.

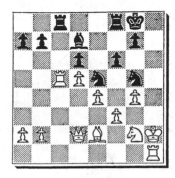

324A. White moves. He has *the pattern for a discovered attack* by moving his Knight from QB4 and unmasking the action of his Rook on the Queen's Bishop file. The most effective way is (apparently) *1 KtxKP*, attacking Black's Queen and thereby winning his Knight on KKt3. But Black coolly allows his Queen to be captured! There follows *1 ... KtxKt!; 2 RxQ.*

324B. Black moves. Do you see *the Knight fork pattern* on which he has relied? Both Black Knights attack the vital point KB6! So: **2 ... Kt(Kt4)xP**ch (capture of the BP by the other Knight will also do the trick); **3 BxKt** (parrying the fork), **Ktx B**ch (renewing the fork!) winning White's Queen and leaving Black a piece ahead. Note how attacking weapons are used for defense!

DEFENSE BY DECLINING A SACRIFICE

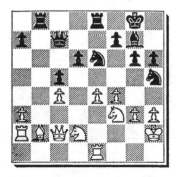

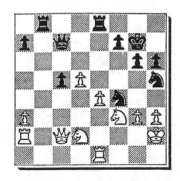

325A. **Black moves.** He tries an unsound sacrifice in order to penetrate into the heart of the adverse King-side position. He plays *1 . . .* **P—Q4,** to open the diagonal leading from his Queen to the hostile King. There follows *2* **BxB, KxB;** *3* **BPxP** and now *3 . . .* **Kt(K3)xP?** He hopes for *4* **PxKt, QxP***ch;* *5* **K—R1, Q—Kt6** with good attacking chances.

325B. **White moves.** He defends with a subtle retreating move: *4* **Kt—B1!** Thus he guards the precious Knight's Pawn, allows his Queen to shift to the threatened zone—and leaves the sacrificed Black Knight dangling with *no retreat!* Later, at his leisure, White will capture the doomed Knight, with Black bereft of attacking chances. Witty play!

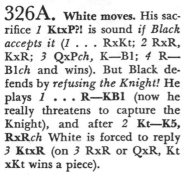

326A. **White moves.** His sacrifice *1 KtxP?!* is sound *if Black accepts it* (*1* . . . RxKt; *2* RxR, KxR; *3* QxPch, K—B1; *4* R—B1ch and wins). But Black defends by *refusing the Knight!* He plays *1* . . . **R—KB1** (now he really threatens to capture the Knight), and after *2* Kt—K5, RxRch White is forced to reply *3* KtxR (on *3* RxR or QxR, Kt xKt wins a piece).

326B. **Black moves.** Relying on *forcing* moves, he continues *3* . . . KtxKt; *4* QxKt, Q—B7! with a two-fold mating threat at KKt7. White's reply is again forced (*5* Q—Kt8ch would be meaningless); but after *5* Q—Kt3 White's Queen is *overworked!* Black *undermines* it with *5* . . . BxPch, forcing *6* QxB so that *6* . . . QxR wins the exchange.

ATTACK AND COUNTERATTACK

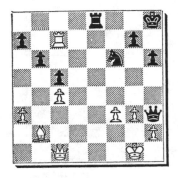

327A. White moves. In this exciting position, he plays *1* **BxKt**, expecting *1* . . . PxB; *2* Q—Kt1 (threatening *3* Q—R7 mate), P—B4; *3* Q—Kt2*ch* (or *3* Q—R1*ch*) followed by mate. Black therefore defends with *1* . . . R—K7, threatening *2* . . . Q—Kt7 mate. Passive defense by White will lose: *2* Q—B1?, QxRP mate. Therefore he continues the attack: *2* R—B8*ch!*

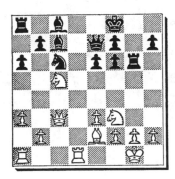

328A. White moves. His combination wins the exchange, but fails to take Black's resources into account. *1* KtxRP is based on the notion that it forces *1* . . . PxKt when *2* QxKt wins a Pawn. Instead Black has the crafty rejoinder *1* . . . RxKt!; *2* Bx R (this is what Black wants: the removal of the Bishop from K2), PxB; *3* QxKt. White has won the exchange.

329A. White moves. The opening thrust *1* Kt—B5 is difficult to parry. It strikes again at Black's *pinned* Knight and also threatens a "family check" *Knight fork* at Q6. If Black tries *1* . . . KtxKt; *2* RxR, Kt —Kt6 (*Knight fork* as defense); *3* R—R7*ch*, K—Kt1; *4* R(K4)—K7 and White remains the exchange ahead. But there is a satisfactory Knight fork *defense* to the Knight fork *threat*: *1* . . . Kt—B5!

327B. **Black moves.** What to do? If he tries flight with 2 . . . K—R2, then *3* Q—Kt1*ch*, P—Kt3; *4* R—R8 mate. So Black tries the alternative *2* . . . **QxR;** but now he has given up the defense of his King Rook Pawn, whose other defender is *pinned and paralyzed!* The sequel: *3* Q*xP ch*, K—Kt1; *4* Q*xP* mate. An exciting, fascinating battle of wits!

328B. **Black moves.** He is the exchange down, yet he has a sly move which turns defeat into victory. The move is *3* . . . **B—Kt2!**, with a *skewer attack* on White's Queen and on the Knight behind the Queen. If now *4* QxB(Kt7)*?*, BxP*ch* (*discovered attack*) wins the Queen. After *4* Q—B3, BxKt (White's Knight Pawn is *pinned*), Black has two Bishops for a Rook, with an easy win.

329B. **White moves.** His opponent's amazing *unpin* prevents the Knight fork at Q6 but leaves his Rook at K5 unprotected. However, after *2* RxR, Kt—Q7*ch*; *3* K—R1, Kt xR Black has regained the Rook by a Knight fork, and in turn prevents White's Knight fork at Q6! A further delightful point: if now *4* R—K1 (Black's Knight must not move), R—B2! as White's *first rank* cannot be deserted by *5* RxKt??

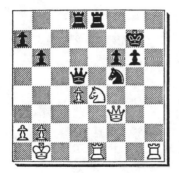

330A. White moves. He sacrifices a Rook to force a "family check" *Knight fork*. Yet Black wins, as he has a brilliant defense by means of Knight forks! The play goes *1* R—R7*ch?!*, KxR!; *2* KtxP*ch*, K—Kt2! If now (see Diagram 330B) *3* KtxQ, Rx R*ch*; *4* K—B2, KtxP*ch* winning the Queen and the game by a Knight fork.

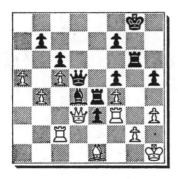

331A. Black moves. He pushes *1* . . . P—K7, giving his Bishop more scope and threatening to win by *2* . . . R—K6; *3* Q—B4 (if *3* RxR??, QxP mate), RxR; *4* QxQ, R—B8*ch* etc. White fights back with *2* RxP. Black presses on the King file with *2* . . . Q—K3, threatening *3* . . . Rx R. White has no additional defense for the Rook at K2, nor can he move it away. Therefore: *3* RxR, PxR.

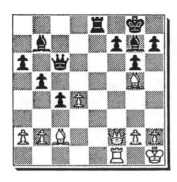

332A. Black moves. As White's Queen seems chained to the defense of his King Knight Pawn (to prevent mate), Black reasons that the Queen is *overworked* and that *1* . . . BxP is feasible (if *2* QxB??, QxP mate). Also, if *2* Q—Kt3, R—K7 wins quickly. But White, surprisingly enough, plays *2* QxP*ch,* and after *2* . . . K—R1, he seems to have a hopelessly lost game.

330B. **White moves.** He tries *3 KtxRch,* expecting a King move. But Black, after studying all checks and captures, counters with *3 . . . Rx Kt!* After *4 QxQ* (what else?), he wins artistically with *4 . . . RxRch; 5 K —B2, Kt—K6ch* followed by *6 . . . KtxQ.* A delightful example of resourceful defensive play.

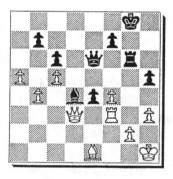

331B. **White moves.** His only defense is counterattack, now that his own Queen and Rook are exposed to *double attack.* He plays *4 P—B5,* leaving Black in the same predicament, and hoping for the simplifying *4 . . . PxQ; 5 PxQ* etc. Instead there comes *4 . . . PxR!* (*study every capture!*); *5 PxQ, PxPch; 6 K—R2, P— Kt8(Q)* mate! Black looked one move further ahead.

332B. **White moves.** There seems to be nothing better than *3 Q—B3,* but then Black wins easily with *3 . . . QxQ; 4 PxQ* (forced—why?), *R —K7.* Instead, White defends with *a surprise move: 3 B—K4!* After *3 . . . QxB* (not *3 . . . RxB??* with a *vulnerable first rank: 4 Q—B8* mate) White has a perpetual check: *4 B— B6ch, BxB; 5 QxBch, K—Kt1; 6 Q— B7ch, K—R1; 7 Q—B6ch* etc.

21 : ILLUSTRATIVE GAMES

Theory looks well on paper, but does not amount to any-
*thing without practice—*JOSH BILLINGS
You will never avoid oversights by grim determination;
*what is needed is a trained eye—*PURDY
*Thou shalt not shilly-shally—*NIMZOVICH

ONCE UPON A TIME there was a Great Man who wrote
and talked a great deal about chess. He had a weighty plati-
tude for every situation and a "trick move" for every opening. One of his admirers adopted the recommended line in
a game, received a severe trouncing for his pains, and com-
plained, more in sorrow than in anger, that he had been
led astray. The Great Man had a ready answer. *"That,"* he
said disdainfully, "is the move we *recommend.* But *this* is
the move we *play."*

In the present volume, there has been no cleavage between the moves that are recommended and the moves that
are played. Every diagram has been taken from practical
play; the moves given actually took place, or else they were
plausible variations of "what might have been." In every
case, the atmosphere of the living game, with its crises of
attack and defense, thrust and parry, threat and counter-
threat, trap and ruse, plan and refutation—all these elements have been faithfully recorded and reproduced.

The games on the following pages round out our survey
of basic attacking motifs. As you play over the games, you
will see how these motifs and patterns constantly enter into
practical play; how they determine the outcome of the
contest; how vital a role they perform, even when they are

206

only considered, without being applied in the game. The winners in these encounters play "winning chess" because they have mastered the basic patterns of tactical play. These patterns have become part of their thoughts: thinking about chess is thinking in terms of the patterns.

ANALYZING A COMBINATION

Before we go on to the Illustrative Games, it will be useful to review the combinative process.

We know that it is easy to analyze a combination when its component moves are *violent*. For such moves require *instant* attention. A check, for example, compels your opponent to drop everything, and get his King out of check. Again, your opponent *must* recapture to regain lost material: an extra piece—or even a Pawn—will generally be enough to win the game.

It is important, then, to look for these *moves of violence*, to try (mentally) every check or capture. Even the absurd-looking moves deserve a moment's consideration; they may turn out to be surprise key-moves to a winning continuation. *Forcing moves make up combinations, and combinations decide games.*

Let us analyze the position in Diagram 333 in the light of these remarks. In this way we shall see what happens when we apply the formula of trying every possible check and capture. You have the White pieces and you are to analyze as though you were playing a game—without moving a piece. At first glance, it

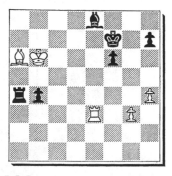

333. **White moves and wins.**

seems that you have a familiar winning pattern here: *double attack*. The idea is: you can play *1* RxB (*a move of violence*). Then, after *1* . . . KxR, you play *2* B—Kt5*ch* followed by *3* BxR and win.

But wait! Have you picked your opponent's best reply? *Does he perhaps have a move of violence at his disposal?* Indeed he has! You play *1* RxB, expecting *1* . . . KxR. But suppose he interrupts your combination and plays one of his own, requiring your *immediate* attention?! Suppose that he answers your *1* RxB with *1* . . . RxB*ch. His* move of violence is more forceful than yours: you must get out of check at once. You capture his Rook, and he captures yours. You continue with *3* K—Kt5, but the reply *3* . . . P—Kt6 crushes you: his Passed Pawn must queen.

Was your combination unsound? Yes, *in the form in which you played it.* If your combination is to succeed, you must prevent him from interrupting it by taking the Bishop *with check.* Retrace your steps. You adopted the first *capture* you saw. Now try *checks. 1* B—B4*ch* looks good, because Black's King has only one move *to guard his Bishop: 1* . . . K—B1. *Now,* by means of *2* RxB*ch* you capture his Bishop—*with a check.* There follows *2* . . . KxR (no time for anything else!); *3* B—Kt5*ch*, K moves; *4* BxR winning easily, as Black's Passed Pawn is no threat.

QUEEN'S INDIAN DEFENSE

New York State Championship, 1940

WHITE: *I. Chernev*   BLACK: *W. A. Cruz*

1 P—Q4	Kt—KB3
2 Kt—KB3	P—QKt3
3 P—B4	B—Kt2
4 Kt—B3	P—K3

If Black now plays some indifferent move such as 5 . . . P—Q3?, White advances powerfully with 6 P—K4 with a formidable center (6 . . . BxP?? would lose a piece by 7 KtxB, Black's Knight being *pinned*).

5 . . . .   B—Kt5

An interesting reply: the Brazilian Champion follows the same line of reasoning: White's Knight at QB3 is in turn *pinned*, thereby nullifying its control of K4.

5 B—Kt5

The *pins* begin! Black has fianchettoed his Queen's Bishop so that it will bear down on the long diagonal. He is particularly interested in controlling the vital center square known as Black's K5 or White's K4.

White of course wants to dispute his opponent's control of the important square, which we shall call K4. White therefore *pins* Black's Knight at KB3, *which is one of the pieces controlling K4.*

Recalling as we do that *a pinned piece is a paralyzed piece,* we can see how White's last move helps to neutralize his opponent's grip on K4.

Now the otherwise desirable 6 P—K4 cannot be played, for then Black simply replies 6 . . . BxP! taking advantage of the *pin* on White's Knight at QB3.

White therefore decides to consolidate his position *by giving his pinned Knight additional support*—a useful precaution.

6 **R—B1   P—KR3**

"Putting the question"—the
Bishop must make up his mind.
If 7 BxKt, QxB and Black has
gained in development and has
an easy game. If 7 B—B4 or 7
B—Q2 the pin is gone and again
Black has a fairly easy time of it.

White therefore tries the most
logical but riskiest course: *main-
taining the pin.* Why risky? Because White's Bishop may run
into a case of *no retreat.*

7 **B—R4!?   P—KKt4**
8 **B—Kt3   Kt—K5**

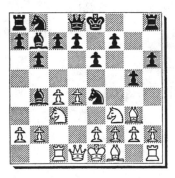

By means of energetic play,
Black has driven the Bishop into
a blind alley, *gotten rid of the
pin,* freed his King's Knight for
action and *intensified the pin* on
White's Queen Knight.

Apparently Black's affairs are
in a flourishing state, but there is
one drawback: he has weakened
his King-side Pawns by their advance. If White can regain the
initiative later on, the weakened
sector will be a vulnerable target
for counterattack.

9 **P—K3   . . . .**

Thanks to White's sixth move,
his *pinned* Knight, which is
doubly attacked, is amply
guarded.

9 . . . .   P—KR4

Threat: *10* . . . P—R5; *11*
B—K5, P—KB3 and the Bishop
has *no retreat!*

Black now anticipates the
following: *10* P—KR3 (to make
room for the Bishop), BxKt*ch;*
11 PxB, KtxB; *12* PxKt, Q—K2
followed by . . . P—Q3, . . .
Kt—Q2 and . . . O—O—O.
Black would then have a fine
game and White's position
would be riddled with Pawn
weaknesses.

But White resorts neither to
passive defense nor to deep pre-
occupation with Black's threats.
White prefers a different course:
counterattack!

10 **P—Q5!   P—R5**

On with the dance: he reckons
on *11* B—K5, P—KB3; *12* B—

Q4, P—K4 and the Bishop is trapped (*no retreat*).

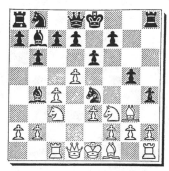

11 Q—Q4!   . . . .

White's first aggressive move, curtly changing the picture with kaleidoscopic suddenness. Black's Bishop at Kt2 is blocked out of action. Meanwhile Black is menaced with *double attack* against his Rook at KR1 and Knight at K5.

11 . . . .   P—KB3

A sad comedown from his previous aggressive policy. If instead *11 . . . Kt—KB3*, the *pin 12 B—K5* wins a Pawn at the very least.

12 QxKt   PxB
13 BPxP   . . . .

It is generally desirable for Pawns to capture toward the center. In this case, however, *13 RPxP* was out of the question because of the *pin* by Black's King Rook.

Nevertheless White is satisfied

with the text. His opening of the King Bishop file creates a valuable avenue of attack.

13 . . . .   Kt—R3

Note that Black's King Pawn is *pinned*. This is also true of White's Queen Pawn.

14 Q—Kt6ch   K—B1

White has penetrated into his opponent's game. The Black King is more insecure than ever.

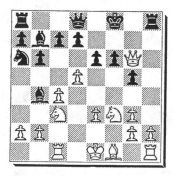

15 B—K2   Q—K2
16 O—O   . . . .

White's Knight at QB3 has been *unpinned*, and may come into the game very quickly. Black therefore decides to remove the Knight.

16 . . . .   BxKt
17 RxB   . . . .

Now Black sees new troubles in the offing. The threat is *18 KtxP*, a murderous move utilizing the open King Bishop file for a decisive pin.

If Black tries *17 . . . Q—B2*, then the simple *18 QxQch, KxQ; 19 KtxPch* wins (*still pinning!*). Even stronger, however, is *the exploitation of the pin* with *18 Kt—K5!*

17 . . . .   **R—KKt1**

Where should White's Queen retreat?

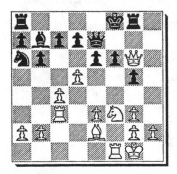

18 **Kt—K5!**

No retreat is necessary! The impertinent Knight cannot be captured, as Black's King Bishop Pawn is pinned.

Meanwhile *19 RxPch* is threatened; this would leave Black the victim of a quick mate. Note how Black is handicapped by not having his pieces properly developed.

18 . . . .   **R—Kt2**

He must not capture the Queen, for after *18 . . . RxQ; 19 KtxRch* (*Knight fork!*) and White's material advantage decides easily in his favor.

After *18 . . . P—KB4* White would have had a choice of many good continuations, the strongest doubtless being *19 B—R5.*

19 **Q—R6!**   *. . . .*

By *pinning* Black's Rook, White made it an *overworked piece*. He now threatens to win the Queen by means of the *Knight fork 20 Kt—Kt6ch.*

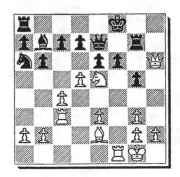

19 . . . .   **K—Kt1**

If *19 . . . Q—K1; 20 Q—R8ch, R—Kt1* (or *20 . . . K—K2; 21 QxRch*); *21 QxPch* and mate next move.

Or *19 . . . K—K1; 20 B—R5ch, K—Q1; 21 Q—R8ch* leading to mate.

20 **Kt—Kt6   Q—Q1**

Amusing would be *20 . . . Q—B2; 21 Q—R8 mate* (*a smothered mate of sorts!*).

If *20 . . . RxKt; 21 QxRch* and White wins easily.

21 **Q—R8ch   K—B2**

Black prays for the exchange of Queens.

22 Kt—K5*ch*   . . . .

Still taking advantage of the *pin*, White forces the King to K2 (*removal of the guard*), so that 23 QxR*ch* will be possible. As Black cannot prevent this, he resigns.

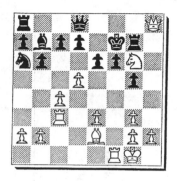

RUY LOPEZ

Pernau, 1910 (Simultaneous Exhibition)

WHITE: *A. Nimzovich*   BLACK: *Ryckhoff*

1 P—K4	P—K4
2 Kt—KB3	Kt—QB3
3 B—Kt5	Kt—B3
4 O—O	P—Q3
5 P—Q4	. . . .

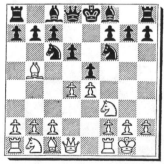

Black's position is somewhat cramped, and the fact that his Knight at QB3 is *pinned* adds to

the generally uncomfortable effect.

The simplest defense is 5 . . . B—Q2, *unpinning* the Knight. Instead of this, Black embarks on a dangerous adventure with:

5	KtxKP?
6 P—Q5	. . . .

The Pawn attack on a *pinned piece*—always a precarious situation for the defender. Luckily Black can escape the worst if he plays with great care.

6 . . . .   P—QR3!

The only correct reply: *defense by counterattack*. The point is that if now 7 B—R4 (to maintain the pin), then 7 . . . P—QKt4 ends the pin and at the same time saves the piece—again *defense by counterattack*.

But White has a more dangerous reply.

7 B—Q3!   . . . .

Now both Knights are attacked; can both be saved? They can, but the solution is not an easy one.

7 . . . .   Kt—B3?

Wrong! He retreats to threaten *a Pawn fork,* but the idea is unsound.

To maintain material equality, he should have tried 7 . . . Kt—K2; 8 BxKt, P—KB4; 9 B—Q3, P—K5. In this way he would have won back the lost piece, although after *10* R—K1, PxB (or . . . PxKt); *11* QxP the *pin* on the King file would have assured White a winning game.

8 PxKt   P—K5

Now he has the *Pawn fork;* but he discovers that it is foolish to conduct tactical operations on the open King file while *his King is still on that line.*

9 R—K1!   . . . .

The *pin* saves the piece for White.

9 . . . .   P—Q4

The KP needed support.

10 B—K2!   . . . .

A subtle move. *10* B—B1 would have saved the piece, for if then *10* . . . B—K2 *(unpinning); 11* KKt—Q2 removes the remains of Black's Pawn fork possibilities.

10 . . . .   PxKt

11 BPxP! . . . .

11 B—Kt5*ch* also wins, but the text is prettier.

11 . . . . **BxP**

A delightful point is *11 . . .* PxB; *12* PxR(Q) and Black cannot capture the Queen at his Q8 because his King's Pawn is *pinned!*

White's *queening threat* has been parried, but it served its purpose: it opened an important diagonal.

12 **B—Kt5 mate!!!**

Nimzovich's procedure here in closing the King file (*10* B—K2!) in order to open it later for

Final Position

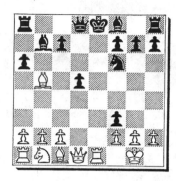

a lethal double check and mate, reminds us of the play in Diagram 254A, where Black opened a line of communication in order to close it!

QUEEN'S INDIAN DEFENSE

Played by Correspondence, 1928

WHITE: *A. Berlin*   BLACK: *F. Aspengren*

1 P—Q4	Kt—KB3
2 P—QB4	P—K3
3 Kt—QB3	P—QKt3

| 6 PxP | PxP |

The diagonal is closed now—
a deceptive state of affairs.

Black would do better to *pin* the Knight by *3 . . . B—Kt5*; for after the text White has two strong continuations: (a) *4 P—K4*, monopolizing the center; or (b) *4 P—Q5*, blocking off the action of the Black Bishop which is coming to QKt2.

| 7 B—Kt2 | P—B4? |

| 4 Kt—B3 | B—Kt2 |
| 5 P—KKt3 | . . . . |

Black's last move was a mistake, partly because he is neglecting to bring out his forces; partly because Pawn contacts result in open lines, which is favorable to White here because he has more pieces in play; partly because the Queen's Pawn is deprived of Pawn protection—something that Black may come to regret.

| 8 O—O | PxP? |

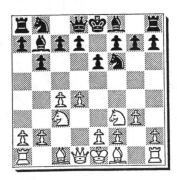

Again neglecting his development and bringing White's pieces to more aggressive posts.

| 9 KKtxP | B—K2 |
| 10 Kt—B5! | . . . . |

White plans to "fianchetto" his King's Bishop (play it to KKt2). As soon as he castles, this Bishop will be guarded by the White King and therefore in a more secure position than the Black Bishop whom he faces on the long diagonal.

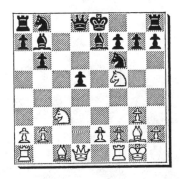

| 5 . . . . | P—Q4 |

Even at this early stage, White has a won game. The Queen's Pawn is *pinned* (why?) and is therefore an immobile target. It is attacked three times and defended three times, but it cannot be guarded by a Pawn (the most secure form of protection).

The further course of the game illumines the insecurity of protection by pieces.

10 . . . .   O—O

White can now win a Pawn by *11 KtxBch,* relying on the fact that after *11 . . . QxKt* one of the defenders of the Queen's Pawn has been drawn off. But he has an even more elegant method.

11 KtxQP!   . . . .

A neat tactical device makes this move possible despite the fact that the Queen's Pawn *seems* to be defended as many times as it is attacked.

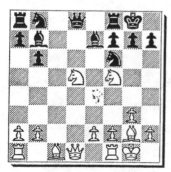

11 . . . .   KtxKt

Practically forced.

12 BxKt   . . . .

12 . . . .   Q—Q2?

Black's best chance was *12 . . . BxB; 13 QxB, Kt—R3* with a Pawn down (but not *13 . . . QxQ?* allowing the *Knight fork 14 KtxBch* which wins a piece. We see now that Black's Queen Pawn was vulnerable because his Queen was *overworked*).

13 BxB   QxB

Black's Queen still guards the Bishop, but White's *surprise move* in reply wins more material.

14 **Q—Q5!!**   **Resigns**

What pathetic helplessness! If *14* . . . QxQ the *Knight fork 15* KtxB*ch* wins a piece. If Black tries to trap the Queen by *14*

. . . Q—B2 then *15* QxR (*15* KtxB*ch*, QxKt; *16* QxR is even simpler), Kt—B3; *16* QxKt!, Qx Q; *17* KtxB*ch* still echoes the same theme!

QUEEN'S GAMBIT DECLINED

New York, 1913

WHITE: *F. J. Marshall*   BLACK: *H. Kline*

1 P—Q4	P—Q4
2 P—QB4	P—K3
3 Kt—QB3	Kt—KB3
4 Kt—B3	B—K2
5 B—Kt5	QKt—Q2
6 P—K3	O—O
7 R—B1	P—QKt3

An old-fashioned defense which was popular during the gay '90s. The defense later went out of style because it generally results in a weakened Queen-side structure for Black. How this comes about, and how it can be exploited, are drastically set forth in the later play.

8 PxP	PxP
9 Q—R4	B—Kt2
10 B—QR6!	. . . .

The first point. After the exchange of Bishops, the white squares on the Queen-side become "holes" and vulnerable to occupation by White.

10	BxB
11 QxB	P—B3?

This Pawn still remains a target for attack on the Queen's Bishop file. More promising, therefore, was *11* . . . P—B4.

12 O—O	Kt—K5

He seeks freedom by exchanging pieces.

13 BxB	QxB

Even at this early stage, White has a winning continuation!

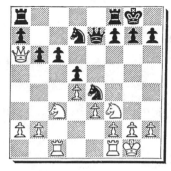

14 Q—Kt7!   . . . .

The attack on the weak
Queen's Bishop Pawn cannot be
parried. Thus *14* . . . QR—B1
allows the same continuation as
actually happens in the game;
14 . . . Q—Q3 allows *15* KtxKt,
PxKt; *16* RxP and wins; while
14 . . . P—QB4 loses by *15* Ktx
Kt, PxKt; *16* Kt—K5 (*exploiting
the pin*), KR—Q1; *17* Kt—B6,
the *Knight Fork* winning the exchange.

14 . . . .   **KR—B1**
15 KtxP!   . . . .

A winning *pin!*

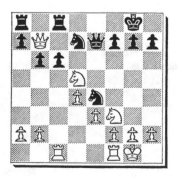

15 . . . .   **Q—Q3**

He must guard the Queen's
Bishop Pawn. It is clear that if
15 . . . PxKt; *16* RxRch, RxR;
17 QxRch, Kt—B1; *18* R—B1
and White wins easily.

16 RxP!!   . . . .

"The most unkindest cut of
all."

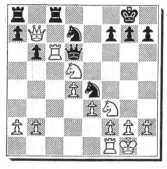

Black resigns, for if *16* . . .
QxR; *17* Kt—K7ch wins the
Queen by a *Knight fork.* If *16*
. . . QxKt; *17* RxRch wins the
Queen by *discovered attack.*
Finally, if *16* . . . RxR; *17*
QxRch, Kt—Kt1 forced; *18* Kt—
K5, R—B1; *19* Q—Kt7!, R—B1;
20 Kt—K7ch!, K—R1; *21* QxKt
(K4), QxKt(K2); *22* Kt—Kt6ch
again winning the Queen by
discovered attack. Even speedier
is *21* KtxPch!, RxKt; *22* Q—
B8ch and mate in two more
moves (*vulnerable first rank*).

RUY LOPEZ

Hastings Christmas Tournament, 1927–28

WHITE: *E. G. Sergeant*   BLACK: *L. Steiner*

1	P—K4	P—K4
2	Kt—KB3	Kt—QB3
3	B—Kt5	P—QR3
4	B—R4	Kt—B3
5	Q—K2	B—K2
6	P—B3	P—QKt4
7	B—Kt3	O—O
8	O—O	R—K1
9	P—Q4	. . . .

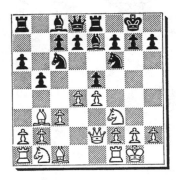

White's game is much freer, and his pieces are posted more aggressively. From this it follows that: (a) if new lines are opened, White will benefit accordingly; (b) Black should avoid such line-opening.

9 . . . .   PxP?

Wrong: he permits the opening up of the game. Correct was the patient *9 . . . P—Q3* keeping the position closed.

10 P—K5!   . . . .

In order to drive away the Black Knight now at KB3—traditionally the castled King's best defender. Black fights back, using a *pin*:

10 . . . .   B—B4

So far, so good. Black is momentarily holding his own, for if *11 PxKt??*, RxQ etc. But White parries cleverly.

11 Q—Q3!   Kt—KKt5

The better part of valor; if instead *11 . . . KtxP?; 12 KtxKt, RxKt; 13 PxP* and the *double attack* by means of the Pawn fork wins a piece.

12 Kt—KKt5!   . . . .

Instead of playing *12 PxP* (which is quite good), White

chooses an even sharper method. He now threatens *13 QxPch* or *13 BxPch.*

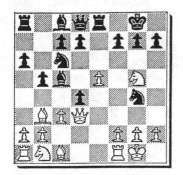

12 . . . .   Kt(Kt5)x KP

13 QxPch   K—B1

The Black King's castled position has been shattered, his security is gone.

14 PxP   . . . .

A *Pawn fork* to gain time.

14 . . . .   BxP

15 Kt—QB3   . . . .

White threatens *16 Kt—Q5* (blocking the flight of Black's King) with a quick win.

15 . . . .   BxKt

16 PxB   Kt—K2

There is nothing better. If *16 . . . Q—B3; 17 B—R3ch, P—Q3; 18 P—KB4, Kt—B5; 19 QR—K1!* with a winning attack.

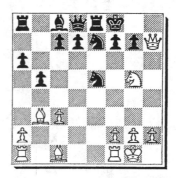

17 P—KB4

White could also play *Q—R8ch,* as this move is superfluous.

17 . . . .   Kt—B5

If *17 . . . Kt(K4)—Kt3?; 18 KtxP* with a *smothered mate* of the Black Queen!

18 Q—R8ch   Kt—Kt1

19 Kt—R7ch   K—K2

20 QxP   . . . .

White threatens *21 BxKt (removing the guard),* PxB; *22 Q—K5* mate.

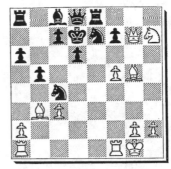

20 . . . .   P—Q3

Stops White's threat, but the Black King is not happy.

21 P—B5   . . . .

Threatens 22 B—Kt5*ch*, winning Black's Queen, as his King Bishop Pawn is *pinned*.

White can win in various ways, for example by the *Knight fork* 23 Kt—B6*ch*. But the method he chooses (concentrating on the *pin*) is certainly the most forthright.

23 BxKt(B4)   PxB
24 QR—K1   . . . .

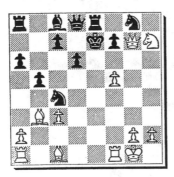

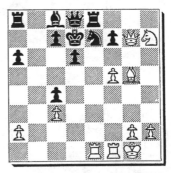

21 . . . .   K—Q2

Preventing the *skewer* check.

22 B—Kt5   . . . .

Not a skewer now, but it leads to a pin which forces Black's early surrender.

White threatens the *Knight fork* 25 Kt—B6*ch* followed by 26 KtxR, QxKt; 27 RxKt with crushing gain of material.

24 . . . .   K—B3
25 QxP   . . . .

Black resigns, for the *pin* is beyond endurance; if *25* . . . K—Q2; *26* P—B6 or *26* Kt—B6*ch* wins easily.

Brief as this game is, it has provided us with examples of the pin, double attack, smothered mate, skewer, and Knight fork. These resources were exclusively White's property; hence his quick victory.

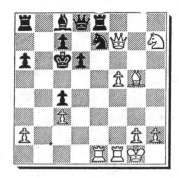

QUEEN'S GAMBIT DECLINED

U. S. Championship Preliminaries, 1938

WHITE: *F. Reinfeld*   BLACK: *J. W. Collins*

1	Kt—KB3	Kt—KB3
2	P—Q4	P—Q4
3	P—B4	P—B3
4	Kt—B3	PxP
5	P—QR4	B—B4
6	P—K3	P—K3
7	BxP	QKt—Q2
8	Q—K2	. . . .

With his fourth move, Black "gave up the center"—his center Pawn *captured away from the center*. The long-range consequence is that White may be able to establish a strong center by playing P—K4—now that Black's Pawn has disappeared from Q4.

If White succeeds in playing P—K4, Black's pieces will be barred from the following squares (reckoning from Black's side of the board): KB4, K4, Q4 and QB4. White's last move (8 Q—K2) is intended to force P—K4; Black's next move parries that threat.

8	. . . .	Kt—K5
9	O—O	B—Q3
10	KtxKt	BxKt
11	Kt—Q2	B—Kt3
12	P—K4	O—O

White has succeeded in carrying out his strategical goal (setting up a strong center with P—K4). To get some benefit from this advantage, he proceeds to apply tactical methods.

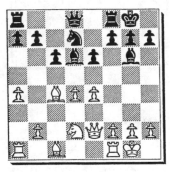

13 P—B4! . . . .

Black's pieces do not have access to the center squares. They are therefore likely to be poorly placed. This is particularly true of the Bishop at KKt3.

Hence *13 P—B4!* threatening to win the unfortunate Bishop by *14 P—B5 (no retreat).*

13 . . . . **B—B2?!**

A courageous player, Black decides to play for complications. If instead *13 . . . Kt—B3?* (to answer *14 P—B5* with *14 . . . B—R4*); White has the *Pawn fork 14 P—K5* winning a piece.

The only real alternative was *13 . . . P—KR3*, creating a retreat for the Bishop at KR2— where, however, it would be badly out of play.

14 P—B5!   **PxP**
15 PxP   . . . .

Apparently the Bishop is lost: *no retreat.* But Black has an ingenious defense:

15 . . . .   **R—K1!**

Defense by counterattack!

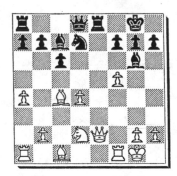

If White removes his Queen from attack, his advantage will disappear. For example: *16 Q—Q3, B—KR4* saving the Bishop and threatening the *double attack . . . B—K7. 16 Q—B3* looks better, but then comes *16 . . . Q—R5!* (*with the mating pattern of Diagrams 307A and 307B*); *17 P—KKt3, QxQPch* followed by *17 . . . Kt—K4* and again Black has the initiative by counterattack.

This is all very puzzling: White started out with a considerable strategical advantage; yet he stands to lose his whole advantage because of tactical difficulties.

16 Kt—K4! . . . .

A surprising move (White voluntarily *pins* himself and exposes the Knight to *double attack*). The sequel had to be very closely calculated.

Still directed against the *pinned* Knight. The idea is if *17* KxB, Q—R5ch (*double attack*); *18* K—Kt1, RxKt followed by . . . B—R4.

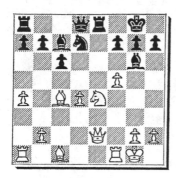

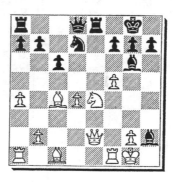

If now *16* . . . B—R4; *17* QxB, RxKt; *18* BxP*ch*, K—R1; *19* Q—B3 retaining a strong initiative.

16 . . . Q—R5 leads to very complicated play, the main line being *17* P—KKt3 (he has to prevent the mate), QxKt; *18* QxQ, RxQ; *19* PxB, RxP; *20* PxBP*ch*, K—B1; *21* P—QKt3 with a winning game.

Most remarkable is the fact that the *pin* by *16* . . . Kt—B3 is worthless! Relying on *priority of check*, White replies *17* Ktx Kt*ch*. After *17* . . . PxKt; *18* Q—Kt4 the *pin* on the Bishop wins a piece for *White*. On *17* . . . QxKt White has the fascinating reply *18* PxB! (*defense by counterattack!*) remaining a piece ahead no matter how Black plays!

16 . . . .   BxP*ch*?!

17 K—R1!! . . . .

Defense by refusal of a sacrifice. The fact that both Black Bishops are *en prise* enables White to extricate himself from even the most precarious situations.

Apparently *17* . . . Q—R5 is crushing, but it is defeated by the surprising reply *18* B—KKt5!

If then *18 . . . QxKt; 19 QxQ,
RxQ; 20 PxB, B—Q3; 21 RxP*
and wins. Or *18 . . . Q—R4;
19 P—KKt4* etc. Of course, *18
. . . QxB; 19 KtxQ* is quite
hopeless for Black, as he loses
too much material.

On *17 . . . B—R4; 18 QxB,
RxKt* White has a problem at
first sight. If *19 KxB?, R—R5ch*
with *double attack*, or *19 QxB?,
R—R5 pinning* the Queen. However, the Bishop can be taken
safely after *19 B—KKt5!* or
(even more simply) *19 QxBPch*.

17 . . . .   **B—B2**

Desperately hoping for *18
PxB??*, when *18 . . . Q—R5ch*
leads to mate as in Diagrams
307A and 307B.

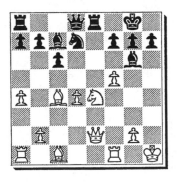

18 **B—KKt5!** *. . . .*

Decisive! Black cannot play
18 . . . P—B3 (his King Bishop
Pawn is *pinned*). If his Queen
moves off the attacking diagonal,
19 PxB at last becomes feasible.
If *18 . . . QxB?; 19 KtxQ, RxQ;
20 BxR* winning Rook and
Bishop.

Finally, if *18 . . . RxKt; 19
BxQ* (the simplest), *RxQ; 20
BxB!, R—QB7; 21 PxB, RxB;
22 PxBPch, K—R1* (if *22 . . .
K—B1; 23 B—Q6* mate); *23
QR—K1* and Black is helpless
against *24 R—K8ch (queening
combination* plus *vulnerable last
rank*).

18 . . . .   **Kt—B3**
19 **BxKt**   **PxB**
20 **PxB**   *. . . .*

The end of the trail for the
Bishop.

20 . . . .   **PxP**
21 **KtxP***ch*   **Resigns**

A final convincing Knight
fork!

Black's stubborn and ingenious defense created a great number of intricate tactical problems.

Solutions to Quiz Problems

PINS (pages 22–23)

25. Black wins a piece with *1 . . . QxKt.* White cannot recapture because of the *pin.*

26. White *pins* the Queen with *1 B—Kt5.* Black's Queen is lost.

27. White produces a winning *pin* by means of *1 KtxB, KtxKt; 2 Q—R3* and Black's Knight cannot be saved. Also possible, but not quite so strong, is *1 RxB, KtxR; 2 Q—R3.*

28. First White forces Black's King into a *pin: 1 KtxB, KxKt.* Then comes *2 P—K4,* winning the *pinned* Knight.

29. White has the winning *pin 1 R—B8.* Black loses his Queen.

30. *1 . . . RxP* is not advisable, for then *2 Q—QKt4 pins* and wins the Black Rook.

BREAKING A PIN (page 28)

37. Black *breaks the pin* with *1 . . . B—Q5ch.* The advance of White's King Bishop Pawn was a blunder, for it made the Bishop check possible.

38. Black *breaks the pin* with *1 . . . Kt—B6!* If then *2 RxR??, R—Kt8 mate!*

39. By means of the *counterpin 1 . . . B—B4* Black wins the White Queen.

40. Black *breaks the pin* with *1 . . . KtxKt!* with counterattack on White's Queen. *1 . . . Kt—Kt4?* loses a piece: *2 BxQ, KtxQ; 3 KtxKt* etc.

KNIGHT FORKS (pages 48–49)

72. White wins a piece by *1 QxKt(7)ch!, KxQ; 2 Kt—Q6ch* followed by *3 KtxQ.* The *forking* check does the trick.

73. Black's Bishop is pinned. Hence the *forking* check *1 Kt—Kt6ch* wins the exchange.

74. *1 RxKt!* leaves Black without a good move. After his Queen retreats (if *1 . . . QxR* the *forking* check *2 Kt—B5ch* is decisive), there follows *2 Kt—B5ch, K—Kt1; 3 P—R3!* White is now safe against a possible *. . . R—R8ch,* and he can play *4 QxP* with withering effect.

Diagram **75.** By playing *1* **RxB!** White wins a piece; for *1* . . . **PxR** allows the murderous forking check *2* **Kt—K7***ch* winning the Black Queen.

76. *1* **Kt—B6***ch forks* Black's King and Queen. Note that Black's Bishop is *pinned*: if *1* . . . **BxKt;** *2* **QxQ***ch* etc.

77. The violent *1* **RxKt***ch!* is decisive. As Black's Queen is *pinned,* he must reply *1* . . . **KxR,** allowing the *forking* check *2* **Kt—B5***ch*.

DOUBLE ATTACKS (page 66)

106. The *double attack 1* **Q—Kt4***ch* wins Black's Bishop.

107. *1* **R—Kt5** (*double attack*) wins the Knight. Black's Queen can no longer guard the *loose piece*.

108. Black begins with *1* . . . **P—KKt4.** After White's attacked Bishop moves away, Black completes the *Pawn push* with *2* . . . **P—Kt5** winning a piece.

109. The *double attack 1* **Q—K4!** wins Black's Bishop because of the mate threat at Black's KR2.

DISCOVERED ATTACKS (page 79)

128. The *discovered attack 1* **RxP***ch!* wins Black's Queen by uncovering the action of White's Bishop against the Queen.

129. *1* **Kt—B6!** attacks Black's Queen and at the same time creates a *discovered attack* on the Knight at Black's Q4. As Black will naturally want to save his Queen, he has no time to salvage the Knight on Q4.

130. The *discovered attack 1* . . . **BxP***ch!* wins White's Queen. Another triumph for the principle of *priority of check*.

131. The *discovered attack 1* . . . **BxKt** wins a piece, as it exposes White's Queen to attack by the hostile Rook at Black's Q1.

DISCOVERED CHECK (page 84)

139. The *discovered check 1* **P—Q5***ch* wins Black's Queen.

140. The *discovered check 1* **Kt—Q6***ch* wins Black's Queen.

141. The *discovered check 1* . . . **P—B5***ch* wins the Bishop at White's Q3.

DOUBLE CHECK (page 88)

Diagram 146. *1 . . .* **RxQ** permits *2* **R—B8** with *double check* and mate! Neither check can be parried, because White is giving check at K5 *and* B8.

147. Black mates in two moves with *1 . . .* **B—Q6**ch (*double check*); *2* **K—K1** (interposition is impossible), **R—B8** mate.

THE OVERWORKED PIECE (page 98)

161. *1 . . .* **RxB**ch undermines White's *overworked* Rook at B1. After *2* **RxR, QxR** Black is a piece ahead.

162. By playing *1 . . .* **RxKt** Black demonstrates that White's Queen is *overworked*: if *2* **QxR??, QxP** mate.

163. White proves that Black's Knight at QB3 is *overworked* by playing *1* **BxKt.** After *1 . . .* **KtxB;** *2* **QxB** White is a piece ahead.

164. White has two ways of exploiting the *overworked* state of Black's Queen. The most obvious is *1* **BxKt, QxB;** *2* **RxB** winning a piece. The other way is *1* **RxB, QxR;** *2* **BxKt** followed by Q—Q2—R6, anticipating the mating pattern of Diagram 290, p. 178.

REMOVING THE GUARD (page 109)

180. White *removes the Black Queen's guard* with *1* **BxKt,** at the same time providing his own Queen with needed protection.

181. *1* **KtxP**ch *removes the guard*: after *1 . . .* **KtxKt;** *2* **RxR** White has won the exchange.

182. White's King guards his Queen. Black *removes the guard* with *1 . . .* **B—B7**ch! There follows *2* **KxB, QxQ**ch etc.

183. White's King guards his Queen. Black *removes the guard* by *1 . . .* **R—Kt8**ch!; *2* **KxR, QxQ.**

"NO RETREAT" (page 117)

199. Black's Knight has *no retreat* to a safe square. Hence *1* **P—KR4** wins the Knight.

200. *1* **P—KB5** leaves Black's Bishop with *no retreat*. There follows *1 . . .* **P—R4;** *2* **R—Kt3, B—Kt5;** *3* **P—R3!** winning the trapped Bishop.

Diagram 201. If Black's Knight at KB3 is attacked, it has no retreat. *1* P—K5 therefore wins the Knight.

202. After *1* Kt—K3, Black's Queen has *no retreat*: every possible move it can make exposes it to capture. The Queen is lost.

THE SKEWER (page 126)

213. By playing *1* QR—B1, White *skewers* Queen and Bishop, winning a piece. *1* KR—B1 is less clear because of *1 . . .* Q—Kt7.

214. White wins Black's Queen by the *skewer* attack *1* R—R7*ch*. Note that the defense *1 . . .* R—B2 is not feasible.

215. Black wins the exchange by the skewer *1 . . .* B—QR3. White must not try to save the exchange with 2 Kt—QKt5, for then *2 . . .* P—B3 wins a piece.

216. *1 . . .* Q—K8*ch* forces White's King onto the King Bishop file. This makes possible the *skewer 2 . . .* Q—KB8*ch,* winning White's Queen.

QUEENING COMBINATIONS (page 137)

229. White *removes the blockader* with *1* B—B6*ch*. After *1 . . .* K—B2 there comes 2 P—K8(Q)*ch* winning Black's Queen by a skewer!

230. Black gets rid of the Bishop by means of the Pawn fork *1 . . .* P—K5*ch*. After 2 BxP, KtxB; *3* KxKt, P—B7 the Pawn *must queen.*

231. The simplest way for White to win is *1* QxR!, PxQ; *2* P—R6 and *the Passed Pawn cannot be stopped!*

232. Black simplifies with *1 . . .* QxKt*ch* (*1 . . .* RxKt achieves the same effect); 2 QxQ, RxQ; *3* RxR and now he *can promote his* Passed Pawn: *3 . . .* P—Kt8(Q)*ch.*

THE VULNERABLE FIRST RANK (page 148)

246. The quickest way to remove the guardian of Black's first rank is of course *1* QxR*ch!* Then after *1 . . .* KxR; 2 R—K8 mate demonstrates *the vulnerability of Black's first rank.*

247. By playing *1* R—Q1! White proves that *Black's first rank is vulnerable.* Black cannot play *1 . . .* RxP?? be-

Diagram   cause of 2 R—Q8 mate in reply. But after such moves
              as *1 . . . K—B1* or *1 . . . P—Kt3*, the reply *2 R—
              Q8ch* is crushing.

248. White exploits Black's *vulnerable first rank* by playing
     1 QxRch!, KtxR; 2 RxKt mate.

249. White's exploitation of Black's *vulnerable first rank* is
     based on *1 R—K1!* An amusing sequel: *1 . . . R—
     Kt1?!; 2 RxQ* (not *2 QxR??, QxR* mate on *the vulnera-
     ble first rank!*), *RxQ; 3 R—K8* mate.

COMBINED OPERATIONS (page 173)

279. White wins by *1 R—Kt8!* (*a pin*), *QxR; 2 Kt—K7ch*
     (*Knight fork*).

280. *1 B—Q6ch!* (not *1 BxPch?, RxB*) is a *discovered attack*
     on the Black Queen. *1 . . . K—Kt2* is forced, but then
     the *Knight fork 2 Kt—R5ch* wins the Queen after all.

281. The *double attack 1 P—Kt4!* wins a piece, for if *1
     . . . QxP; 2 R—KKt2* or *R—KKt1* pins the Queen.

282. White creates a pin with *1 R—K1*. To save the Knight,
     Black must play *1 . . . P—Q3*; but then the double
     attack *2 Q—Kt5ch* or *2 Q—R4ch* wins the Bishop at
     Black's QR4.

DESIGN FOR CHECKMATE (page 189)

310. *1 Q—R6* leaves Black without any way of preventing
     Q—Kt7 mate. (See Diagram 288.)

311. *1 R—R3ch, K—Kt1; 2 R—R8* mate. (See Diagram
     292.)

312. *1 Kt—K7ch, K—R1; 2 QxP* mate. (See Diagram 284.)

313. *1 Q—R6ch, K—Kt1; 2 Q—R7* mate. (See Diagram
     286.)

About the Authors

IRVING CHERNEV *has written many successful chess books, including the best-selling chess primer* Invitation to Chess, *which he co-authored with Kenneth Harkness. Chernev is a deep student of the game, but he writes about it in a witty and entertaining manner; his scholarly approach is combined with a light touch.*

FRED REINFELD *is credited with being the world's most prolific chess writer. He has also defeated many of America's leading masters in tournament competition. After annexing the Intercollegiate Championship in his undergraduate days, he won the New York State Championship twice and subsequently became the titleholder of both the Marshall and Manhattan Chess Clubs.*

BOTH *Chernev and Reinfeld have a phenomenal knowledge of chess literature. They can (and do!) spend hours discussing the details of hundreds of master games without bothering to consult any texts or sources. Their love for the game is enormous, and, they hope, contagious.*

Printed in the United States
By Bookmasters